I
DIDN'T
SIGN UP
FOR THIS

I DIDN'T SIGN UP FOR THIS

NAVIGATING LIFE'S DETOURS

AARON SHARP

DISCOVERY HOUSE
PUBLISHERS®

I Didn't Sign Up for This: Navigating Life's Detours

© 2012 by Aaron Sharp

Discovery House is affiliated with RBC Ministries, Grand Rapids, Michigan.

Requests for permission to quote from this book should be directed to: Permissions Department, Discovery House Publishers, P.O. Box 3566, Grand Rapids, MI 49501, or contact us by e-mail at permissionsdept@ dhp.org

ISBN 978-1-57293-513-6

Interior design by Michelle Espinoza

Library of Congress Cataloging-in-Publication Data

Sharp, Aaron.
I didn't sign up for this: navigating life's detours / Aaron Sharp.
    p. cm.
Includes bibliographical references.
  ISBN 978-1-57293-513-6
1. Bible. O.T. Kings, 1st, XIX—Criticism, interpretation, etc. 2. Christian life—Biblical teaching. 3. Elijah (Biblical prophet) I. Title.
  BS1335.6.C43S53 2012
    222'.5306—dc23   2011053336

Printed in the United States of America
Second printing in 2012

To my lovely and talented wife, Elaina. Of all the ways that you are God's blessing in my life, and they are almost infinite, none has proven to be so pronounced and important as having you on all my detours. On this book alone you have played the role of cheerleader, editor, and theological sounding board. Your encouragement, determination, and gracious love are why, after His Son, you have been God's greatest gift to me.

CONTENTS

THE STORY OF ELIJAH

Late Ninth Century B.C.
Mount Carmel, Israel

Three groups of people made their way up the mountain.

In the first group were thousands of regular, everyday people. They were making the short trek, ready to see one of the ancient world's greatest pieces of theater—a showdown between rival prophets. Many of them were trying to decide exactly what to believe and just who to worship. These people were not royalty, nor were they priests. They were shepherds, farmers, and fishermen. If nothing else, these Israelites anticipated a good show.

Interspersed within the first group was another group, this one numbering 450 strong. The colorfully adorned men in this second group were prophets of the Canaanite fertility god Baal. Worship of Baal, who was typically pictured as a bull, had been practiced in this area long before the Israelites had conquered the Promised Land. Now with the worship of the one true God at an all-time low in Israel, these priests had done much to lead the Israelites astray.

Worship of this pagan god revolved around fulfilling the desires of the worshipper. The ultimate act of worship was when the worshippers worked themselves into a frenzy of passion, with the prophets and priests functioning as sacred prostitutes. Worshipping Baal meant excitement, thrill, and feeding one's own appetites and desires.

The third group of people was not really a group at all. It was one single, solitary man. As was his custom, the man wore a hairy garment and a leather belt. He was not only the underdog in that day's contest, he was also the reason for the gathering. Every step that his sandals took crackled on parched ground. And every crackle reminded him and everyone else that he was the one who had caused all of this trouble. He had prophesied that it would not rain in the land of Israel until he said that it would. Then God commanded him to leave the land of Israel. Now, three years later, he had returned, and the dry and barren mountain was testament to the authenticity of his prophecy.

The prophet Elijah made his way up the formerly beautiful Mount Carmel to take on the prophets of Baal, one versus four hundred fifty. So much had changed during the three years that Elijah had been gone. King Ahab and Queen Jezebel had murdered God's prophets, and the drought had brought on a severe famine that was felt heavily in Ahab's capital city of Samaria. When the prophet had reappeared, King Ahab had called him the "Troubler of Israel." Elijah challenged Ahab to gather the nation and the priests of Baal to meet him on Mount Carmel. The meeting would show, once and for all, that God was all-powerful and that Baal was an empty shell of a dead and uncaring idol.

Once Elijah, the king, the prophets of Baal, and the assembled crowd had settled in on a plain just below the mountain's peak, Elijah began to speak. The prophet's voice bellowed across the natural amphitheater created by the mountain's features as he challenged the people of Israel to choose whom to follow, Baal or the God of Abraham, Isaac, and Jacob. He directed that two oxen be brought and that the 450 prophets of Baal be given their choice of cattle to sacrifice. Each would prepare their own ox for sacrifice. Then whichever deity sent fire from heaven to consume the sacrifice would be the one true God.

The prophets of Baal went first. A careful observer of the priests slaughtering the bull and placing it upon the altar would realize that they already had a major problem. They worshipped a god of fertility, the one responsible for thunder, rain, and agriculture. Yet the priests were performing their sacrifice after three years of drought and famine. In fact, the very mountain on which they now stood had been a national symbol of vibrant beauty (Song of Solomon 7:5; see also Isaiah 35:2), but now, after three years without rain, it was an icon of futility. The prophets performed their rituals with much music, dancing, and gyrations, but the entire morning passed without any word from Baal, or so much as a spark from heaven.

By noontime, with the act of Baal's prophets growing tiresome for the assembled crowd, the lone prophet of Yahweh became more and more openly adversarial. Despite the fact that this large contingent of colorfully adorned priests had continuously chanted, "O Baal, answer us" for several hours, they had seen no evidence of their deity. Elijah heckled them, saying, "Call out with a loud voice, for he is a god; either he is occupied or gone aside, or is on a journey, or perhaps he is asleep and needs to be awakened." Elijah had the audacity to suggest that Baal was asleep, or possibly even away on a trip. No doubt this taunting of the prophet's theological nemesis both shocked and delighted the crowd that was by this point bored.

The priests of Baal responded to the eccentric prophet's ridicule by taking their worship to extreme measures. Since their deity was not responding to their chants and calls for actions, the prophets now began to slash and cut themselves. Cries rang out and blood gushed over their vividly colored outfits as the prophets grew more and more desperate for Baal to act. This disturbing behavior continued until the middle of the afternoon when Elijah finally had had enough.

Against a backdrop of his opponents' pitiful cries for action, bloody and beaten by their own desperate hands, Elijah called the people to gather around. He took the time to choose twelve stones and to construct an altar, which he promptly surrounded with a trench. After the painstaking process of constructing his altar and digging the trench, Elijah killed the ox. After the animal had breathed its last, he cut the ox into pieces and laid the bloody pieces on the altar to be sacrificed. Then, in a move that shocked the crowd as much as his earlier taunting, Elijah commanded that twelve pitchers of water be poured on top of the ox and the altar. After a three-year drought, the spectators must have gasped when so much water was used that it even filled up the trench.

Then Elijah prayed. Though his prayer was relatively short, it must have felt like he prayed for an eternity. There was no delay in what happened next. Unlike Baal, whose priests had sought his help for hours, Elijah's God saw no reason to delay.

Fire exploded from heaven and streaked across the evening sky. The fire blazed closer and closer until it impacted Elijah's makeshift altar as if God had punched the earth with a fiery fist. The fire completely consumed the ox, the water, and even the stones. Where once had stood an altar, was now just a smolder.

The solitary man in the hairy garment wasted no time in completing the triumph. Elijah turned from the smoking ashes that proclaimed his God's victory and commanded the people to seize the bloody and defeated prophets of Baal. He then meted out the punishment God had decreed for false prophets—all 450 prophets were slain. There was no trial. They were all guilty and they paid the price.

As an encore, Elijah told King Ahab, the most prominent worshipper of Baal, to take his chariot down the mountain because it was about to rain, for the first time in a very long time. A great rain did come, but not before the prophet outran Ahab's chariot down the mountain.

Few human beings in history have ever had a better day than Elijah did on Mount Carmel. Words such as *legendary*, *historic*, and *awesome* only begin to tell the story of the showdown on Mount Carmel. Had newspapers existed at the time, editors would have had strokes trying to come up with a headline that would do it justice. With apologies to a young shepherd boy who one day slew a giant and eventually became king, the feat brought about by Elijah was only rivaled in Israelite history by Moses' parting of the Red Sea. Years later young Jewish boys would urge their fathers, "Tell me about the day with Elijah on the mountain again!"

But the prophet's great day quickly turned into a very dark night. In a stunning turn of events, fire from heaven became a distant memory for the prophet almost before the embers of that blaze had grown cold.

INTRODUCTION

A few years ago my girlfriend (now wife) and I spent a Fourth of July weekend with her family at their lake house on Eagle Mountain Lake. We had not been dating long, and it was my first time to visit them at the lake. Much of the weekend was spent on WaveRunners, objects almost as unfamiliar to me as the members of my wife's family. We were out on the WaveRunners one morning when I was told to take the WaveRunner I was on and follow someone else, also on a WaveRunner, to a dock across the lake.

At the time I was more than a little distracted talking to my girlfriend, and so I did not pay close attention to the person I was supposed to follow, or even where my destination was. After a minute or so I took off across the lake, chasing the person to the dock. I could see him in the distance, and so I followed, and followed, and followed, until finally, after having crossed the width of the lake, I arrived at a marina and realized, much too late, that I had followed the wrong person.

I was now alone on an unexpected detour on a lake as unfamiliar to me as the Sea of Galilee. Actually, I might have known the Sea of Galilee better, because I had at least seen pictures of it in the back of my Bible. I did not know even the basic shape of Eagle Mountain Lake. I had no cell phone, and I had not memorized my girlfriend's phone number on the off chance I could find a phone.

Despite the predicament in which I found myself, I thought that I could find my way home. I remembered that I could see the lights of a baseball field from their back porch. Surely I could find a baseball field along the shore somewhere. Once I found that, it would be a breeze to navigate the rest of the way. Besides, this was Texas—how big could the lake be, anyway?

Minutes turned into hours. I traversed the lake trying to find my way back with little success. At one point I ran out of gas and had to dock my vessel at the home of a nice couple who helped me as much as they could. I did not know what city my girlfriend's family house was in, as several bordered the lake, so they gave me a full tank of gas and I headed back out onto the lake. The hot July Texas sun had turned my usually pale skin into a shade of tomato red. My sunburn hurt, I was exhausted, I was embarrassed, I was frustrated, and with the sun slowly beginning to descend, I had no idea where I was or what lay in front of me.

Eventually, however, I found my way home. They had sent a search party out for me, but I managed to find my way back on my own, saving a tiny (very, very tiny) sliver of self-respect. To this day, her family still talks about my afternoon on the lake, and I laugh about it now, telling everyone that I know the lake better than all of them put together. But, if I am honest, that is not the only time in my life that I have been on a detour. The other times did not involve lakes, WaveRunners, or sunburn, but the change in my course was just as unexpected, just as fearful, and just as frustrating.

There was the time that I got the call from my parents telling me that my mother had cancer. There was the year after college when I struggled to discern God's will for my future. There was the time in seminary when I hurt my knee, requiring a surgery that took all of my savings for school and then some. There was the huge conflict in my extended family that may never be resolved, my graduation from seminary with no job prospects, my wife's miscarriage, and the unexpected loss of a close friend. There was my layoff, then my wife's, and then mine again.

All of these circumstances left me feeling much the same as I did that day on the lake. At least with my aquatic adventure I can look back on it and laugh, but I cannot say that about all the other detours. Nor can I explain why these difficult times occurred, or what God was doing in my life through them. Some of them are, at least this side of heaven, unexplainable. I could make up a reason for their happening, but I do not truly know.

If we are honest with ourselves, we have to admit that we all end up on these unexpected detours from time to time. Maybe it is bad news from the doctor, a pink slip, an argument, or any number of things, but we can easily find ourselves in situations where we feel like I did that day on the lake. Often we begin to question ourselves, God, and life itself when our planned course changes direction. We wonder why our problems seem to get bigger by the minute and worry about how long it will be before we can find our way home.

Fortunately for us, the characters of the Bible are no strangers to detours. Job's detour—the sudden loss of his children, possessions, and health—was quite possibly unlike any before or since. Abraham's detour of being unable to produce children left him feeling so out of sorts that he slept with his wife's servant in an attempt to accomplish God's will on his own. Joseph went from being his father's favorite child to a slave, sold into slavery by his brothers, and then to a falsely accused prisoner. David experienced detours that left him so exacerbated that he exclaimed:

> *How long, O Lord? Will You forget me forever?*
> *How long will You hide Your face from me?*
> *How long shall I take counsel in my soul,*
> *Having sorrow in my heart all the day?*
> *How long will my enemy be exalted over me?*
> *(Psalm 13:1–2)*

The list of detoured lives that grace the pages of Scripture could go on and on. It includes men and women, Jew and Gentile, old and young. This is important for us to note because often when we are in the midst of a detour we feel like we are the only one who has experienced anything like the heavy fog in which we are living. If you are not careful, you can conclude that you must be the only person who has ever felt like life is closing in on you and nothing is going right. The question of the prophet Habakkuk, "How long, O Lord, will I call for help, and You will not hear?" (1:2), will be on your lips, and it is important to know that you are not the first person to have thought those thoughts and said those words.

Perhaps no biblical figure has taken a more disappointing detour than the prophet Elijah. Elijah bursts onto the stage of biblical literature from out of nowhere. After the death of Solomon, the nation of Israel split into two kingdoms, with the northern nation of ten tribes going by the name of Israel and the southern two tribes, Benjamin and Judah, going by the name of Judah. As you read about these events in the book of 1 Kings, you see a pattern develop in Israel. The kings "did evil in the sight of the Lord," and they got progressively worse. By the time you read about King Omri, who "did evil in the sight of the Lord, and acted more wickedly than all who were before him" (1 Kings 16:25), you are convinced that this nation must have hit rock bottom. Then you read about Omri's son, Ahab:

Now Ahab the son of Omri became king over Israel in the thirty-eighth year of Asa king of Judah, and Ahab the son of Omri reigned over Israel in Samaria twenty-two years. Ahab the son of Omri did evil in the sight of the Lord more than all who were before him. It came about, as though it had been a trivial thing for him to walk in the sins of Jeroboam the son of Nebat, that he married Jezebel the daughter of Ethbaal king of the Sidonians, and went to serve Baal and worshiped him. So he erected an altar for Baal in the house of Baal which he built in Samaria. Ahab also made the Asherah. Thus Ahab did more to provoke the Lord God of Israel than all the kings of Israel who were before him. (1 Kings 16:29–33)

Chapter 16 of 1 Kings ends with a summary of the depravity of King Ahab and his queen, Jezebel. Between the two of them, they were the most wicked monarchy in Israel. They openly defied God and His laws for the nation.

Chapter 17 then begins with an unexpected contrast: "Now Elijah the Tishbite, who was of the settlers of Gilead, said to Ahab, 'As the Lord, the God of Israel lives, before whom I stand, surely there shall be neither dew nor rain these years, except by my word'" (1 Kings 17:1). From out of nowhere, in the midst of deep wickedness, Elijah storms into the story proclaiming that there will be no rain for three years. His appearance is sudden. We had no evidence that anyone was willing to stand for God, much less openly oppose the most wicked of kings, but that is exactly what Elijah does.

Elijah follows up this prophecy by obeying God's directions to live near a stream, with ravens bringing him bread and meat to eat each morning and evening. After this he travels to the town of Zarephath where he works miracles, including the raising of a widow's son from the dead. Then, when the drought is in its third year, God instructs Elijah to go back to Israel and confront King Ahab. Elijah obeys God and what results is a famous confrontation between Elijah and 450 prophets of the false god Baal. By the end of the confrontation, Elijah has called down fire from heaven, the 450 prophets of Baal have been executed, Elijah has outraced Ahab's chariot down the mountain, and the storms are rolling in.

One would expect after such powerful acts that Elijah's encore would be out of this world. Yet, in the words of A. W. Pink, "In passing from 1 Kings 18 to 1 Kings 19 we meet with a sudden and strange transition. It is as though the sun was shining brilliantly out of a clear sky and the next moment, without any warning, black clouds drape the heavens and crashes of thunder shake the earth. The contrasts presented by these chapters are sharp and startling."[1]

Chapter 18 is a tremendous victory. The sun is shining, birds are singing, and God has shown himself to be powerful and mighty. It looks as though Elijah, through God's power, can do anything. Chapter 19 is a hasty retreat. Storm clouds litter the sky, and suddenly God seems to have disappeared. It looks as though Elijah, God's formerly powerful servant, is weak and vulnerable. It is in the black clouds that drape the heavens, the story of Elijah's detour in 1 Kings 19, that this book resides.

It is important to understand that this book is not a how-to manual. It is not "Seven Steps to Finding Your Way Home." As anyone who has been on one of life's detours will tell you, formulas do not always work. Our culture is fascinated with formulas and programs, but God doesn't work that way. His Bible isn't filled with steps to follow to solve every problem, and this incident in Elijah's life is not a road map for getting to your destination. I cannot guarantee that by reading his story, things in your life will get better. Instead picture Elijah, and his troubles, as a friendly couple at the lake giving someone in the midst of an unexpected detour an extra tank of gas—and sometimes a tank of gas is all you need to find your way home.

ONE

DETOURS AND UNMET EXPECTATIONS

I was in my third year of seminary when I met the woman of my dreams. I still remember what she was wearing the first day we met. We did not even speak that day when we both sat at the same cafeteria table with a group of mutual friends, but I was determined to find out more about her. Over the next few months I slowly got to know this beautiful lady, taking careful mental notes of what kind of a person she was, how she acted, and what she liked. The more I got to know her, the more I found to like. Thankfully, she did not seem repulsed by my presence, so I finally decided the time had come to ask her out on a date. Despite accidentally hitting her in the face with a door earlier in the evening, her answer was yes!

My friends were sure that this was a match made in heaven. She seemed to enjoy my presence, we flirted constantly, and we had much in common. All signs pointed to this being the first of many dates. My friends and I agreed: if there was ever a man whose success on a first date was assured, it was on this date for me.

Once she agreed to go on the date, the work began in earnest. I carefully chose a restaurant for dinner that would be fun, not cheap but not too expensive, with an excellent variety of dishes. I then came up with after-dinner activities that would allow us to talk and get to know each other. The plan was flawless unless I did something stupid, which, let's face it, is always a possibility with me.

I picked her up that evening and we headed to the restaurant for a fantastic dinner. I had pasta while she had crab cakes. At some point in the meal she suggested I try the crab cakes, which I did despite my complete aversion to eating just about anything that comes out of the ocean. To this day she remembers the agonized look on my face as I got my first and last taste of crab cakes.

Our dinner conversation was smooth and we discussed one of the classes we had together—Old Testament History. I mentioned a project that I was considering for the class, and before I knew it we were discussing the possibility of undertaking the project as a team. There could not have been a clearer sign that this date was a home run. Surely, if we were talking about spending dozens of hours together on a project, then she must like me too. I was most definitely on my way to having a girlfriend soon.

After dinner we went to a bookstore where we each picked out books that we would like to read and told the other person why we found those particular books interesting. From the bookstore we made our way to another restaurant where we each ordered a piece of cheesecake and continued our lively conversation. All night long I was the consummate gentleman, opening doors and being attentive. As our night drew to a close, I prepared to return to the dorm to tell all my buddies how I was such a thoughtful, romantic guy and that we would soon be going on a second date.

We pulled up to her apartment building and I walked her to her door. On the way, I casually told my date how much fun I had and how much I would enjoy being able to take her out again. I uttered these words and then waited for the "Sure, that would be great" that I was sure was coming. Instead of agreeing to a second date, however, this lovely woman told me that she was not interested in going on a second date and would really prefer to remain friends.

We arrived at her door. I thanked her for the evening, and then made my way back to my car. Once inside I looked in the mirror—did I have something in my teeth, or something hanging out my nose the whole night? I checked my breath and my armpits—did I smell bad? I mentally replayed the night's events—did she not have fun? I started reviewing our entire history. Did she ever really like me? Was there something wrong with me? Was I a bad date? These and many more questions flew through my mind as I drove back to my dorm. Despite the fact that everything had seemed to go so well, my expectations proved to be the exact opposite of what came to pass. I expected a second date, but instead I found myself watching basketball in the men's dorm by myself. A little less than two and a half years later I would marry that same girl, but at the time I knew nothing of that. All I knew was that real life had veered far off course of my expectations.

Pretty much every human being who is old enough to walk has experienced the disconcerting feeling of unmet expectations. From the first time that another child played with the toy that you wanted, you began to get the concept. You may have been in a room full of toys, but that other kid had the one toy you desperately wanted. You asked for the toy, you demanded the toy, and finally you tried to just take the toy. But instead of getting the toy that you so prized, you got in trouble with an adult.

These first few experiences prepared us for the realization that the world does not revolve around us and that more often than not our expectations will be unmet. Yet, even as adults, we still struggle mightily to remember this concept. This concept is particularly foreign when we are, in our minds, living rightly. We understand that if we live outside of the will of God, bad things will happen to us. Those who choose to live a life of sin will pay the consequences of that sin, and at times their lives will be full of nothing but despair and tragedy. That part of life makes sense to us rationally. Expressions such as "Garbage in, garbage out," "You play, you pay," and "You get what you pay for" are all evidence that humans comprehend the concept that if you live dangerously, then dangerous things can and will happen to you.

We have the same expectation for living rightly—we expect that good living will give us good results. Most of us operate as if the number-one rule for living the Christian life is to do our best to do the right things in the right way. Our to-do lists look like this: go to church, read the Bible, pray, try to be a nice person, love your family, pet the dog, put some money in the plate, pay your taxes, buy lemonade from the little girl on the corner, and try not to get too angry at other drivers (although the occasional scream is perfectly acceptable). We do all of these things and expect that because we have stayed on the straight and narrow path, we will be okay and our good expectations for our life will be fulfilled.

Unfortunately this "play it safe" philosophy does not protect us from disappointment over unmet expectations (nor does it necessarily equate to a healthy, vibrant life for a believer in Jesus

Christ). It may make perfect sense rationally: good life = good expectations fulfilled; bad life = good expectations not fulfilled, but the path that the Bible presents to us is a far more rugged. For instance, take the events that befell the prophet Elijah in the beginning of 1 Kings 19:

> *Now Ahab told Jezebel all that Elijah had done, and how he had killed all the prophets with the sword. Then Jezebel sent a messenger to Elijah, saying, "So may the gods do to me and even more, if I do not make your life as the life of one of them by tomorrow about this time." (vv. 1–2)*

Chapter 18 of 1 Kings closed with Elijah as God's ultimate champion. He was victorious over the idolatrous prophets of Baal, outran a chariot down a mountain, and even kept running seventeen more miles to the town of Jezreel. The biblical record does not tell us what his thoughts were as he ran well over half a marathon, but judging by his reaction beginning in verse 3 of chapter 19, it is probably safe to assume that he did not expect what came next.

Elijah was not the only one to return to the fortress city of Jezreel. King Ahab also returned and was quick to inform Queen Jezebel about the day's events on Mount Carmel. Unlike Ahab, who seemed to be in fear and awe of God's prophet, Jezebel sends a message to Elijah saying, "So may the gods do to me and even more, if I do not make your life as the life of one of them by tomorrow about this time." To the modern reader this was the equivalent of Elijah coming home and finding a severed horse's head in his bed, or seeing his face on Israel's most wanted list. Instead of being a hero, Elijah found himself as public enemy number one, at least as far as the queen was concerned.

One would expect that the man who just killed 450 prophets of a false god would laugh at the threat of one woman. Elijah had just called down fire from heaven; surely he feared no one and nothing. If anything, we would expect more fire from heaven, but the exact opposite happens. Before we get to Elijah's reaction, we must first consider one of the most frequent beginnings of a detour—unmet expectations. Most scholars agree that Elijah's reaction is due to events not playing out as he had envisioned them. Consider a summary of the situation by Ron Allen:

> There are indications in the Elijah narrative that he hoped to eradicate Baal worship and reestablish a united monarchy under the pure Yahwism of Moses. The celebrated contest on Carmel (1 Kings 18) actually began three-and-one-half years earlier in the palace of Ahab, when Elijah said there would be no more rain (17:1). Baal, the fertility god of Canaan, was principally pictured as the deity responsible for rain . . . Surely by all [Elijah's] actions an utter defeat of Baalism had been anticipated. The extermination of the prophets of Baal in mock and grisly sacrifice at the Wadi Kishon (v. 40) seemed to be the final stroke . . . But when Ahab witnessed it and returned to his palace at Jezreel, did he depose his wicked queen? No! He told her of Elijah's victory and did not prevent her from ordering Elijah's execution in reprisal.[1]

Elijah had anticipated that the incredible force with which Yahweh, the one true God, had shown himself to be would bring forth a true and long-awaited revival among God's people and their wicked leaders. After all, had not people fallen on their faces and shouted, "The Lord, He is God; the Lord, He is God"

(18:39)? Surely Elijah expected that the northern kingdom of Israel would turn to God, and possibly the kingdoms of Judah and Israel would be reunited.

Sadly, Elijah's expectation of what was to come could not have been more different from what actually happened. Instead of revival, Jezebel declared vengeance. Instead of becoming a national hero, Elijah became a hunted man. Instead of a king and a queen turning to the one true God in repentance, they stubbornly, rebelliously, and violently lashed out at God's prophet.

Like the prophet Elijah, often our unexpected detours start with unmet expectations. Life takes us in a direction that we did not anticipate and did not desire. The more we look around and try to find somewhere familiar, somewhere that we thought we would be had things been different, the more despairing we can become. Our best attempts to solve the problem of a detour often leave us with a bigger problem rather than a solution.

Understanding that unmet expectations may play a role in our detour is not a solution to our problems. Just knowing this fact will not help you see the situation clearly, but for the fog to lift even a little, we must spend some time thinking about our expectations.

THE PROBLEM WITH OUR EXPECTATIONS

There are three problems with our expectations. First, our expectations are uninformed, if for no other reason than because they involve the future. It is not that we should never consider the future, but that we must realize and anticipate that our expectations may not, and likely will not, be met. Consider the following people and their expectations of the future:

- In 1969 a little known member of the British Parliament named Margaret Thatcher said, "It will be years—not in my time—before a woman will become prime minister." Yes, this is the same Margaret Thatcher who was elected prime minister ten years later.

- In 1943 Thomas Watson, the chairman of IBM said, "I think there is a world market for maybe five computers."

- In casting for the 1964 movie *The Best Man*, about two leading candidates for the presidency of the United States, a young enterprising actor named Ronald Reagan was rejected for the part. Reportedly he was rejected for "not having the presidential look." This is the same Ronald Reagan who took the real oath of office in 1980.

- In 1918 Tris Speaker, a baseball Hall of Famer, felt the need to comment on a move by the rival Boston Red Sox, telling anyone who would listen that, "Taking the best left-handed pitcher in baseball and converting him into a right fielder is one of the dumbest things I ever heard." The player Speaker was referring to—George Herman "Babe" Ruth—finished his career with 714 home runs, a record that stood for nearly four decades.

- Lieutenant Joseph Ives, tasked with studying the Grand Canyon by the U.S. War Department, reported, "Ours has been the first [expedition], and doubtless to be the last, to visit this profitless locality." Today nearly five million people visit the Grand Canyon every year.

We may laugh at these obviously far-off predictions, but if we are honest with ourselves, our expectations for our own lives are just about as inaccurate. Take these expectations, for example:

- I will not have health problems.
- All of my loved ones will live long and fruitful lives.
- I will know when to make a career change.
- I will meet my spouse and fall madly in love by the time I am twenty-four.
- We will have four children.
- My spouse and I will always see eye to eye.

Now some of these expectations may seem a bit silly, and some may be a little more serious, but any one of them can go unmet. Those with some spiritual maturity or life experience will look at the list and say, "Well, obviously those things may or may not happen." And it is definitely true that most of us understand that bad things *might* happen to us, but the point is that even those of us who are not new to the faith or how the world works do not *expect* them to happen. Our expectations are for good health, vibrant relationships, and sunshine in our lives. So, when God allows something tragic or disappointing to come into our lives, most of us are knocked off our feet by it. Our expectations deal with the future, and the future is the one thing that we know very little about.

Second, our expectations are selfish. Pause for a moment and think about your perfect world and what the future would be like if that world happened. Next think of not your perfect world, but a reasonable expectation of life in five to ten years. Now consider how many of your expectations revolved around yourself. Odds are 100 percent of them. Even if you were thinking of the perfect marriage partner, you were thinking of the perfect marriage partner for *you*. You might have thought of the future for your children or grandchildren, but you thought of the future for *your* children and *your* grandchildren. More than likely, nowhere in your imaginings of your perfect world did you think about what life would be like for your friends, much less acquaintances or total strangers. This is a big area where our expectations fail—our expectations revolve around ourselves, but God's plans do not. Our expectations are so often frustrated because while we are focused on ourselves, God is focused on His purposes.

Third, often our expectations are unmet because we have a false perception of who God really is. Our failure to understand exactly who God is and what His priorities include is often one of the biggest factors in our unmet expectations. Consider the following popular, but false, ideas of God and His attributes:

- *God is a slot machine whose sole purpose is to give me what I need or want.* How often do we become frustrated with God because He has not given us what we believe He should have? On this issue, it is easy to point the finger at others, particularly those whose theology disagrees with ours, but all too often this view of God is a problem for all of us. God does desire to give His sincere children the desires of their hearts (Psalm 37:4), but He is not a genie granting our every wish.

- *God is (only) love.* Now, the Bible very clearly states that God is love (1 John 4:8). Love is not simply an attribute of God; it is also part of His essence. Yet we err when we look at God as being only love. Theologian D. A. Carson explains, "Our culture has been purged of anything the culture finds uncomfortable. The love of God has been sanitized, democratized, and above all sentimentalized . . . Today most people seem to have little difficulty believing in the love of God; they have far more difficulty believing in the justice of God, the wrath of God, and the noncontradictory truthfulness of an omniscient God."[2] The prevailing view today is that God is a kind, gentle, grandfatherly being who delights in handing out candy and blessings to people. Unfortunately this is not the God of the Bible. The God of the Bible is love, but He is also holy, righteous, and just.

- *God wants me to be happy.* Happiness is a funny thing. It can come and go so easily. People today, particularly Americans, live their lives in pursuit of happiness. After all, are not we guaranteed the right of doing just that by the Declaration of Independence? Yet God has more important things to accomplish in and through us than mere happiness. God's purpose of using the apostle Paul to spread the gospel was more important than his happiness when he was executed by the Romans (2 Timothy 4:1–8). God's desire to provide for His chosen people was more important than Joseph's happiness when he was sold into slavery and falsely imprisoned (Genesis 45:1–8; Psalm 105:17–19). God's desire to proclaim the truth to His people was more important than Jeremiah's happiness when the king became angry and threw him in a muddy pit (Jeremiah 1:1–10; 38:1–13).

- *God will not give me more than I can bear (alone).* Often when we feel like life has taken a detour it is because we are completely overwhelmed by circumstances. So we cling to the idea that we can make it through these trying times all by ourselves because God would not put more on our shoulders than we can carry. That sounds right, but it misses a large part of God's truth. God routinely puts more on our shoulders than we can carry alone, which is how we realize just how deep our need for God and other people truly is.[3] If we were able to bear the weight ourselves we might never properly acknowledge God, or our brothers and sisters in Christ who are able to bear our burdens with us (Galatians 6:2).

- *God wants Christians to be happy and joyful (always).* This is similar to "God wants me to be happy," but with a slight twist. Some people are under the mistaken impression that God requires that we always present ourselves as happy and joyful, without exception. It is true that we should be full of God's love and the Holy Spirit, and the knowledge of God should give us noticeable joy (Philippians 4:4). However, everyone will experience times of sadness, fear, doubt, and depression, and hiding these emotions is not spiritual. The Word of God reveals that plenty of God's servants had hard times, not the least of which is the instance in Elijah's life about which this book is written. Job experienced severe trials, and his reaction to them was what one would expect: pain, frustration, and anger. We might anticipate that God would respond to Job's negative emotions with a fireball like the one that consumed Elijah's sacrifice. However, the Scriptures tell us that even after Job's emotional outpouring God still accepted him (Job 42:7–9).

DEALING WITH UNMET EXPECTATIONS

We have learned that when life takes an unexpected detour, our first step should be to check our expectations. At this point you may be thinking, "If that is true, then what is the solution for dealing with these unmet expectations?" This is an excellent question and one we will discuss, but first let's change the question around just a bit.

People on detours tend to look for directions and answers, and what they really want is a map that shows the way back home. But I would suggest that God's primary purpose in allowing your journey to take an unexpected detour is not just a lesson in finding your way back to the interstate. As we progress through 1 Kings 19, we will see that this was true of Elijah, and I believe that it is true for most of us as well. Having said that, let's answer a different question: "If it is true that detours are about more than simply finding our way back to our desired path, then what are some guidelines for dealing with these unmet expectations?"

The difference in that question and the one posed previously may seem slight to you, but it is important. On a detour we tend to become even more frustrated and disillusioned looking for solutions. We are focused on the conclusion of the journey, rather than the journey itself. In this circumstance, rather than directions to our final destination, what we really need is extra fuel to continue the journey.

We are unique individuals, and what God is attempting to do in our detours will never be exactly the same from one person to another. Rather than a one-size-fits-all answer, the following principles are meant to function much as additional fuel to keep you going even if your unexpected journey is a lengthy one.

First, when you find yourself on a detour and dealing with unmet expectations, take the time to look for God's purposes instead of your best interests. As fallen creatures, we are inherently selfish, and we live in a world that caters to our desire to fulfill our own desires. So the idea that we should put God's purposes at the forefront is not one that comes easily to us. Certainly it is not our first inclination, but the truth is that what we think are our best interests are not God's top priority. Anyone who has been on a detour for any amount of time has probably gotten tired of having sincere people quote Romans 8:28 to them: "We know that God causes all things to work together for good to those who love God, to those who are called according to His purpose." The verse can be a great encouragement, but often we misread it. The verse says that God "causes" everything to work for good, but it does not mean that only good things will happen to us. Very bad things will happen to us, but God has a purpose and at times my best interests, at least as I understand them, must take a back seat to that greater purpose.

Consider the story of the blind man in John 9. Jesus and His disciples were walking together, and they passed a blind man on the road. The disciples asked what they thought was an insightful question: "Rabbi, who sinned, this man or his parents, that he would be born blind?" (v. 2). They thought his physical impairment must have been tied to a sin, and they wanted to know whose sin it was that caused the blindness. Jesus' answer to His followers, however, turned their theology upside down: "It was neither that this man sinned, nor his parents; but it was so that the works of God might be displayed in him" (v. 3).

Imagine, if you will, the disciples' shock. This man had been unable to see for his entire life (that is one whale of a detour). He had never looked into his mother's or father's faces, or seen a sunset. He had been unable to play with other children as a boy and had struggled with his lack of vision into adulthood. This all happened solely so that God might perform a miracle in His life for all to see. He had done nothing wrong, and his parents had done nothing wrong, yet God allowed this disability so that He could show everyone His power and glory.

If you are on a detour today, you are probably asking yourself and God the most simple of questions: "Why?" You may receive an answer to that question, and you may not. One sure thing is that sometimes God allows our life's path to take tremendous detours so that He can be glorified and we can be equipped to minister to others. If your detour has to do with sickness, it may well be that God wants you to know and understand sickness to minister to others experiencing the same pain. Maybe God has allowed you to feel the pain of depression to help others who struggle with depression. Or it may be that the relational conflict that is causing you such angst may enable you to counsel and minister to others who are going through or will go through similar circumstances. Whatever it is that you are going through, do not discount the impact that your experience can have on others.

Second, even when you are in the midst of a detour, keep your expectations flexible. Too often our expectations are firmer in our minds than is realistic. The apostle James stresses this point in the fourth chapter of his epistle:

Come now, you who say, "Today or tomorrow we will go to such and such a city, and spend a year there and engage in business and make a profit." Yet you do not know what your life will be like tomorrow. You are just a vapor that appears for a little while and then vanishes away. Instead, you ought to say, "If the Lord wills, we will live and also do this or that." (vv. 13–15)

Here, James is not condemning planning for the future, but he is reproaching the attitude of believers assuming that they were able to carry out their plans. They were treating their expectations as if they were a sure thing, when it was all subject to the mind of God, which no one can know.

Though we all have expectations, we must remember that we cannot write our expectations in stone. If we are honest with ourselves, we would have to agree with James's point that we can do nothing on our own. The only reason we make it from one day to the next is because God has provided the breath and life for us. We must approach our expectations with the understanding that we have not been promised tomorrow.

In 2010 the United States military released a Joint Operating Environment report that was commissioned as a look into the future, an attempt to make educated guesses about environments and challenges the military would face over the next twenty-five years. However, the United States Joint Forces Command, which published the report, placed the following statement at the front of the study:

The Joint Operating Environment is intended to inform joint concept development and experimentation throughout the Department of Defense. It provides a perspective on future trends, shocks, contexts, and implications for future joint force commanders and other leaders and professionals in the national security field. This document is speculative in nature and does not suppose to predict what will happen in the next twenty-five years. Rather, it is intended to serve as a starting point for discussions about the future security environment.[4]

Later in the report occurs this sentence: "Predictions about the future are always risky." Throughout its history the U.S. military has learned that their expectations can be far off from reality. The idea that expectations are to be starting points is an excellent way to view them. Expect health, but be ready for sickness. Expect employment, but be prepared to be laid off. Expect good relationships, but be prepared for conflict.

We have looked at Elijah's (and our own) unmet expectations. Next, let us look at what happens when one of God's prophets allows emotion to take over.

QUESTIONS FOR DISCUSSION

1. Which of your expectations for your life have been unmet?
2. What is the most difficult part of dealing with your unmet expectations?
3. What has dealing with unmet expectations taught you about yourself?
4. What have your unmet expectations taught you about how you view God?

TWO

DETOURS AND EMOTIONS

As a child I was afraid of getting in trouble for doing something wrong. This did not always translate into model behavior, but for the most part I abided by the rules, and there were lots of rules. I grew up in a church that tended to emphasize God's holiness at the expense of His grace. Even as a youngster the message was loud and clear—DO NOT BREAK THE RULES! And if for some reason you broke the rules, well then may God have mercy on your soul. Maybe that is why the hush puppy incident is so memorable and, to my own embarrassment, retold so frequently in my family.

One evening, when I was still in my early grade school years, my parents and I went out to a local restaurant for supper. This particular restaurant had an excellent buffet that my parents enjoyed, and they had cheeseburgers, which I enjoyed. We were shown to our table, my beloved cheeseburger was ordered, and my parents went to the buffet for their salads and appetizers. Eventually they both made their way back to the table, grace was said over the meal, and they began to eat while I began my burger vigil. My dad, seeing that I was hungry and knowing that I was fond of hush puppies (though not as much as cheeseburgers), gave me a hush puppy from his plate to tide me over until my meal arrived.

Now my father's action may seem simple enough, but what you must know is that over the buffet was a sign. This sign stated in big, bold letters that there was to be no sharing from the buffet. To a child who could read the sign proclaiming the rule he was violating, eating the hush puppy was as close as I had ever come to being a daredevil. With my mouth watering I picked up my fork and prepared to dissect the forbidden treat on the napkin in front of me.

To understand what happened next it is important to note that, at this point in life, my understanding of physics was in inverse proportion to my understanding of obedience. I anticipated my fork plunging deep into that little sphere of fried goodness, and then transporting that goodness into my eagerly awaiting mouth. The fork, however, did not plunge into the hush puppy. Instead, the hushpuppy, spurred by the strike from the fork, flew off my napkin, over my parents' food, away from our table, and proceeded to strike a waitress in the leg.

As a young rule-abiding citizen I was in absolute horror. Now, as I had heard the verse so often quoted, my sins would truly find me out. I envisioned hours of hard manual labor to pay for my ill-gotten buffet food. Would I be forced to wash the restaurant's dishes? Would I have to clean tables? Would we be kicked out of the restaurant? Would my dad have to pay for an extra meal? All of these thoughts came rushing into my little brain. I had been excitedly anticipating a bite of a wonderful hush puppy, but where there had once been excitement, now there was fear. I had no idea what would come next, and so I acted accordingly, trying to avoid any possible consequences for my lawlessness.

The waitress who had been struck by my fried projectile bent down and picked up the hush puppy. She held it in her hand, and with a smile on her face said, "Was this yours? Let me go get you another one." I panicked like only a small boy can. I quickly reasoned in my head that were she to get me another hush puppy, one that had not bounced across the restaurant floor, then the chances of her discovering our attempt at circumventing the restaurant's rules would be much greater. The best chance I had to get away with our buffet subterfuge was to just keep the first hush puppy, so I responded to her kind request by stammering, "I'll, I'll, I'll just eat that one."

It was hard to tell who was more surprised at my answer, the waitress or my horrified mother thinking about me eating a hush puppy that had just been picked up off the floor. The waitress insisted that she replace it, and so eventually I relented, fearing I had sealed my own fate. Despite my trepidations, however, I was given a fresh hush puppy without any of the consequences that I had imagined. I quickly ate my hush puppy, and ever since my dad has delighted in telling the story of how I tried to convince the waitress to let me eat the hush puppy off the floor.

So what in the world motivated me in that situation? Why would anyone rather eat a piece of food off the floor instead of something hot and fresh from the buffet? Put simply, the situation spun out of control when I let fear take over. Any rational thoughts that I might have had went out the window when I became afraid, and when fear and emotion take over we can do some pretty crazy things.

Unfortunately, we all can attest to the difficulties that arise when we place emotions in the driver's seat of our lives. Maybe it was what you said to the person you love when you were angry.

Maybe it was the time that you decided to start a nasty rumor about someone to get back at them for disappointing you. Or maybe it was the pain of a betrayal that caused you to stop talking to a longtime friend. No matter the emotion, we can all testify to the fact that emotions can take us down the wrong path rather quickly, and this is never more true than of someone on one of life's detours.

Elijah is no exception. We have seen in the first two verses of 1 Kings 19 that Elijah was already dealing with major unmet expectations, and now in the first part of verse 3 we see emotion come into play: "He was afraid and arose and ran for his life." Don't worry about the rest of verse 3—we will get there eventually. Right now just focus on this first part.

Depending on which Bible translation you use, the verse may have a slightly different beginning. The King James Version, the New King James Version, and the Message all begin the verse with the phrase, "And when he saw." The Hebrew words for "fear" and "see" are very similar, and while some manuscripts of the Old Testament contain the Hebrew word for "saw," some contain the word for "was afraid." That is why our many English translations differ as to whether to translate this as "fear" or "see."[1] So is it worth considering that Elijah was not "afraid" necessarily, but that he "saw" what was happening? While I personally lean toward Elijah seeing what happened as opposed to being afraid of what happened, I believe that regardless of whether Elijah was afraid or merely reacting to what he saw around him, both cases exhibit an emotional reaction. The problem may not have been the specific emotion of fear, but a wide range of emotions including frustration and anger. Elijah may have been afraid, but more than likely felt more than one emotion, which is an important realization for anyone on one of life's detours.

Soon after our expectations are unmet, emotions begin to flood our lives. Detours take us somewhere we did not plan to go, and in all likelihood did not want to go. Elijah hoped for a revival, a wave of Israelites and their leaders turning back to the one true God; instead, he got a death threat. No doubt he was afraid, but can you imagine the frustration as Elijah sees his hard work and efforts go to waste? Do not forget, Elijah had spent the three years of drought hiding out by a brook being fed by ravens, and then being cared for miraculously by God at a widow's house in Zarephath. After proclaiming God's punishment of no rain, three years of his life had been spent serving God outside of the nation of Israel and surviving the drought. He reemerged from hiding to confront the king and the false prophets, and then saw God send rain. Now suddenly God has seemingly left him exposed for the queen to squelch the revival and to snuff out Elijah's own life in the process.

A list of the possible emotions that Elijah was feeling could be almost endless. Consider these possibilities for the once mighty prophet:

- Fear of Jezebel.
- Fear that God would not protect him.
- Anger at God for not bringing revival.
- Disgust at his fellow Israelites for not standing up to their king and queen.
- Frustration at God for allowing him to waste the last three years of his life.
- Surprise at the turn of events.

- Sadness at the realization that Israel would most likely be punished by God for sin.
- Remorse at having been so zealous for God when it seemed to be so useless.
- Contempt directed at King Ahab for being so wicked.
- Embarrassment at being such a public figure who God allowed to be threatened.

Elijah's emotional state was more than likely a complex one as he began his detour.

EMOTIONS CAN BE GOOD OR BAD

Human beings are emotional, and emotions, in and of themselves, are not bad. The feelings that you experience as you graduate from college, get a promotion, accept a marriage proposal, or see your grandchild for the first time are all healthy and positive. Even emotions that we normally consider to be negative can have positive effects. If you have ever experienced anger and frustration in a bad relationship, it may have been those emotions that prompted you to make a change. If you have ever felt like a failure in your job, it might have been that emotion that drove you to become a better and more productive employee. Emotions can be good and useful, even those emotions we typically think of as negative.

Emotions also help to define who we are. Sociologist Jack Katz has spent a lifetime studying and writing about human beings and their emotions. You would expect that such a person would describe emotions in matter-of-fact terms, in the same way that your high school biology teacher talked about that frog that you dissected when you were a freshman. Yet Katz refers to the emotions as an "enigma," and as highly individualized. He speaks of emotions that can come in waves, and when he says, "Virtually everyone can recall a song, a sunset, or an appreciation of a child's innocence that brought him to tears even when others at his side were unmoved," he is reminding us that emotions are a part of the human experience, while simultaneously being unique to each person.[2]

Emotions help to define who we are and they can certainly add much to life, but most of us can confirm that they also play tricks on us from time to time. Fear may be the impetus in you fleeing a burning building, but it is also what tells you that you smell smoke during an unannounced fire drill. Is there a fire? No. Is there smoke? No. Yet you and probably several other people can become convinced that you smell smoke because your emotions are beginning to get the best of you.

For the person on one of life's unscheduled detours, emotions can quickly make life much more difficult. If we are not careful, they can threaten to turn a detour into a crash. Emotions such as fear, anger, and frustration—the same emotions that Elijah struggled with—are never more prevalent than when life zigs when we thought it was going to zag. Briefly let us consider what emotions look like when they are out of control, and how to maintain emotional balance when you find yourself on one of life's detours.

OUT-OF-CONTROL EMOTIONS

As we previously discussed, emotions are not intrinsically bad. However, for the person on a detour like the prophet Elijah, emotions can quickly begin to negatively affect actions and choices. Because of this, we need to realize three things about our emotions.

First, our emotions can cause us to become very irrational. That is not to say that rational thought is always good and emotion is always bad, but rather that these two aspects of a person must be balanced. One expert writes,

> These two minds, the emotional and the rational, operate in tight harmony for the most part, intertwining their very different ways of knowing to guide us through the world. Ordinarily there is a balance between emotional and rational minds, with emotion feeding into and informing the operations of the rational mind, and the rational mind refining and sometimes vetoing the inputs of the emotions. Still, the emotional and rational minds are semi-independent faculties . . . reflecting the operation of distinct, but interconnected, circuitry in the brain. In many or most moments these minds are exquisitely coordinated; feelings are essential to thought, thought to feeling. But when passions surge the balance tips: it is the emotional mind that captures the upper hand, swamping the rational mind.[3]

Whenever emotions begin to overtake one's intellect, it usually leads to trouble. Take the emotion of fear, for example. Some people are afraid of snakes. Personally I think this is quite rational, but others would disagree. Then there are those who are afraid of clowns. While I am not afraid of Bozo or Ronald McDonald, enough people have this fear to warrant naming it (coulrophobia). Consider other fears:

- Papyrophobia, the fear of paper
- Metrophobia, the fear of poetry
- Somniphobia, the fear of sleep
- Geniophobia, the fear of chins
- Chromophobia, the fear of color
- Eisotrophobia, the fear of mirrors
- Arachibutyrophobia, the fear of peanut butter sticking to the roof of your mouth
- Pogonophobia, the fear of beards
- Graphophobia, the fear of writing

None of the fears listed above is a rational fear. Paper is nothing to be afraid of—paper cuts maybe, but not just paper. And the fear of peanut butter sticking to the roof of your mouth? That's just bizarre. Irrational fear occurs when emotions and intellect have become severely unbalanced.

Though most people on a detour do not develop strange phobias, they do increasingly struggle to maintain the balance between emotion and rational thoughts. Maybe you are not afraid of peanut butter sticking to the roof of your mouth, but you have become afraid that God cannot provide for or protect you. Maybe you have decided that God wants you to be alone since you do not have a spouse, or even any good friends. Maybe you feel like a failure because you lost your job. Or maybe you think that every time you are detoured, God must be punishing you. Emotions are responsible for these thoughts, not truth.

Second, our emotions can be wildly undependable. Perhaps there is no greater example of this than the modern idea of romanticism. Often in our culture romance is confused for love, but it is vastly different from the biblical description of love given in 1 Corinthians 13. For our purposes we will call our culture's idea of love *infatuation*. Biblically speaking, love is a decision, but infatuation is most definitely an emotional response. People become infatuated easily, and then one day they are no longer infatuated and their relationship loses its foundation. A marriage based upon infatuation will not be characterized by the commitment and sacrifice necessary for it to survive. It will instead be characterized by a strong fire that burns hot, but only for a short time. Whenever that fire goes out, and any couple married for any length of time can tell you that it will, then the infatuated couple is headed for serious problems.

Other emotions are just as undependable. Some days you are happy and some days you are sad, and often there is little rhyme or reason to why you feel that way. Such things as the weather, what we ate for our last meal, traffic, our favorite team's successes or failures, hormonal imbalances, and the time of the day can affect how we feel, and thus our emotional state on an almost minute-by-minute basis. Even smell can trigger a change of emotion. An article in London's *The Times* articulated the often overlooked link:

> Our sense of smell is anchored in the primary olfactory cortex. This part of the brain is yoked to both the hippocampus, which processes memory, and the amygdala, which regulates emotions. This means that aromas that prod the memory also trigger an emotional accompaniment. So we perceive memories triggered by smell as more intense than those provoked by sight or sound. Studies, including several at the Monell Chemical Senses Centre in Philadelphia, have shown that odours can be

useful memory aids. People who are asked to learn in the presence of a distinctive smell, such as violet leaf, show impressive powers of recall when the scent is recreated; they perform better than people whose learning and recall is done in the absence of odour.[4]

Emotions are so easily influenced that the wafting aroma of maple syrup or pine trees can completely change our emotional state of mind. Think of that. In an instant your mood, demeanor, and interaction with other people can all change because your nose picked up on a smell that reminded you subconsciously of something that you might not even consciously remember! If the smell brought back a negative emotion, then it may cause you to have a bad day, with a sullen instead of friendly attitude and a depressed outlook instead of a good one. Of course if the smell sparked a positive emotion, you might go from being down in the dumps to a good mood, from being grouchy to happy, and from being a bad employee to a good employee.

Third, emotions are cyclical. Though it should not be a surprise that emotions are cyclical, most of us rarely think of them in this way. People tend to be in better moods on Fridays, and there is a reason that "having a case of the Mondays" is a popular expression. Consider a 2009 study, published in the journal *Social Psychiatry and Psychiatric Epidemiology*, which concluded that people are most likely to commit suicide in the middle of the week. The study estimated that nearly 25 percent of suicides occurred on Wednesdays compared to 14 percent on Mondays or Saturdays, the two days tied for second-highest suicide rates. Thursdays have the lowest rate, with only 11 percent of suicides. The researchers conducting the study hypothesized that

Wednesday has such high rates because it is the furthest point from the previous and following weekend.[5] While suicide rates may be an extreme example, they demonstrate the effect that a regular occurrence like the day of the week can have on human beings. Clearly emotions are cyclical.

KEEPING EMOTIONS UNDER CONTROL

If our emotions are cyclical and can be irrational and undependable, then how in the world are we ever to survive life, much less one of life's unexpected detours? Even though we cannot control the existence of emotions or how they make us feel, it is possible to maintain a sense of balance, no matter the emotional turmoil we may be enduring.

First, we must take a proper attitude with regard to emotions. Our innate response to emotion is to act. "All emotions are, in essence, impulses to act, the instant plans for handling life . . . The very root of the word emotion is *motere*, the Latin verb 'to move,' plus the prefix '*e-*' to connote 'move away,' suggesting that a tendency to act is implicit in every emotion."[6] The tendency to respond to emotions by acting is natural and at times the right thing to do. However, because emotions can be so unpredictable, we must be very intentional, particularly on a detour, to change the way we think about emotions.

It might be helpful to think of emotions as intelligence reports. In the United States dozens of government agencies sift through stacks of intelligence reports every day. Depending on what is going on in the world, these reports cover such topics as the conflict in Afghanistan, the political situation in Turkey, the drug trade in Colombia, energy issues in Ecuador, the latest Russian aircraft, and the future of leadership in North Korea.

Each of these reports is distilled and passed on, and eventually this intelligence makes its way to the highest levels of the Pentagon and the president's desk in the Oval Office in the form of the President's Daily Brief (PDB). The PDB is usually a ten- to fifteen-page report that the President reviews daily along with top security officials.

Every day hundreds of decisions are made based upon the information contained in intelligence reports. Sometimes the intelligence is accurate and sometimes it is not. Sometimes the intelligence will be interpreted correctly, and other times it will not. The accuracy of the intelligence determines its worth and effectiveness.

On an average day you will have to sort through a wide variety of emotions. Happiness, sadness, anger, frustration, surprise, and a host of other emotions can and will make their way into your everyday life. They provide us information, but that information is not necessarily accurate, and we do not always interpret it correctly. Just because an emotion makes us want to take a particular action does not mean that is what we should do. We may overindulge in what is unhealthy because it makes us feel happy, or avoid important responsibilities because we don't want to feel sad. Sometimes we need to act on considerations other than emotion to do the right thing. When we approach our emotions as information that needs to be sorted through, and discern the best reactions first rather than acting on impulse, then we have begun to gain control.

Second, as believers in Jesus Christ we must always compare our emotions to the Word of God. Emotions can cause us to come to some strange conclusions. For example, based on the emotions that he was feeling, Elijah concluded that he needed to run away and so began his trek to the wilderness. Emotions will do the same to us if we do not have something to stabilize us. Detours are by definition an unexpected part of life's journey. On a detour you find yourself in uncharted territory. Your surroundings are unfamiliar, and you have precious few landmarks that will help you to know which way to go.

In many ways, a detour presents the same problem that travel did hundreds of years ago, before the wonder of highly accurate maps, the Internet, and global-positioning systems. In those times sailors used landmarks on the shore to navigate. However, if they had to proceed in the open ocean, this method of navigation was impossible. They instead turned to another visible place with fixed objects—the sky. Because of its reliance on the heavens, this method became known as "celestial navigation." Travelers could use the sun, the moon, a planet, or any one of fifty-seven different stars as fixed points to navigate safely to their destination.

For the believer on a detour whose emotions are in turmoil, the Word of God can and will function as a fixed point in the voyage through emotions. When emotions tell us that God does not care, the Scriptures tell us that He does (Psalm 55:22). When emotions tell us that God is not in control, the Word tells us that He is (Colossians 1:16–17). When emotions tell us that God has forgotten us, the Bible tells us that he will never leave us (Hebrews 13:5). Like a seafarer of old, so long as we do not lose sight of our fixed point and use it for navigation, we may endure storms, but we will navigate safely.

Third, we must share our emotions with trustworthy people. Even with the proper view of emotions and the realization that we must always navigate emotions by the fixed point of Scripture, we must also filter our emotions through wise and discerning people. Even with an unmovable point such as the Bible, our ability to navigate emotions may still require assistance. Our need for this assistance stems from the fact that our ability to understand God's Word is fallible (even though God's Word is not).

If we are honest with ourselves we have to admit that at times what we see in the Bible is what we want to see. Particularly when emotions are involved, we can decide that God is telling us to do exactly what our emotions are driving us to do. Instead of teaching endurance and to trust in God, our emotions will almost always drive us to panic and attempt to solve problems in our own way and own timing.

Sharing our emotions with others is one of the most difficult parts of maintaining balanced emotions because the last thing we want to do is to admit to another person what we are feeling. We are fearful, and at times legitimately so, that were people to know what we are feeling, we would experience judgment instead of encouragement. That is why we must establish and invest in relationships with those who are spiritually mature. Those people will allow us to express ourselves honestly, without fear of reproach, so that we can work through those feelings. A person who is spiritually mature will allow you to express your anger and frustration without judgment. They will also not allow you to stay in a place where those emotions become the norm.

These relationships will become very important as we see the next step in Elijah's, and often our own, detour.

QUESTIONS FOR DISCUSSION

1. What emotions are the hardest for you to keep in balance?
2. Why do you think that Elijah so quickly lost control of his emotions?

3. Are there particular situations or circumstances that make it difficult for you to control your emotions?

4. God could have made human beings emotionless, but he chose to make us emotional. What does that tell us about our God?

THREE

DETOURS
AND ISOLATION

A few months after my WaveRunner adventure on Eagle Mountain Lake, I was given the opportunity to vacation with my wife's family in Europe. The first stop on our trip was historic London. We visited the Tower of London, toured Buckingham Palace, shopped in Harrods department store, and explored Westminster Abbey. From London we took a train to Paris. While in Paris we went to the top of the Eiffel Tower (no small feat for me considering my fear of heights), toured the lavish Palace of Versailles, saw the Notre Dame Cathedral, and viewed the treasures of the Louvre. After Paris we headed for the final stop on our trip—Amsterdam. We boarded the train in Paris, tired but excited to see another part of the world. We wound our way through the north of France, Belgium, and the Netherlands, eventually approaching Amsterdam.

With seven people and seventeen bags not counting carry-ons, we had developed a unique and efficient method for disembarking from trains. In our system I was the first to get off the train with a large bag. I would set down the bag and turn to be handed another bag, and we would form a sort of bucket brigade unloading bags until finally all of the bags and passengers were off the train.

What happened as we approached Amsterdam is still a matter of debate in the family, though my version of the story is the most accurate, even though it was many years ago. As we approached Amsterdam, someone—I say my future father-in-law, although he denies it—said that the first stop was where we needed to get off the train. The first stop was for the Amsterdam airport. As the train slowed, we stood up and prepared for our departure. As was our system, I grabbed a large suitcase and jumped off the train. I put the bag down and turned, expecting to be handed another suitcase. However, instead of getting another bag handed down to me, the door to the train slammed shut in my face.

As the train began to pull away from the station, I walked beside it pulling the one bag that had been unloaded with me. All I could see through the train door window was my future sister-in-law laughing at my predicament. I walked with the train until the end of the platform, and then it sped away into the dark Dutch night leaving me by myself, save for a large suitcase full of women's clothes.

For a brief moment it was relaxing to be by myself. I am an only child and used to entertaining myself, but that peaceful feeling did not last long. I was thousands of miles from home, it was late at night, my credit cards were not working, and I did not have a phone. To make matters worse, in the Paris train station I had purchased a bottle of Coke, and as a result I had only a few Euros in my pocket, perhaps not even enough to afford a train ticket.

I made my way to the offices of the train company pondering my next move. I concluded that at least I was in the airport. I knew that everyone would have to come back there in a few days. Standing in line for tickets I experienced a lot of emotions. Regret at purchasing that bottle of Coke. Surprise that it had taken them this long to find somewhere to lose me. And loneliness. I knew no one, I could contact no one, and I was as alone as I'd ever been in my life.

My little detour in Amsterdam illustrates something that happens to almost all people experiencing life's detours—isolation. Consider the example of Elijah's detour: "[Elijah] came to Beersheba, which belongs to Judah, and left his servant there" (1 Kings 19:3b). Elijah has seen his expectations unmet by God, he has begun to experience and be led by a wide range of emotions, and now he enters the shadows of isolation. It will become clear in the next few verses that Elijah leaves his servant because he has no intention of returning. He will soon be asking God to take his life, and he is hopeful that God will grant his request.

At best Elijah has little intention of continuing as a prophet of almighty God. As one commentator explained it, "Elijah interprets Jezebel's personal attack on him as the end of his ministry. The prophet's dismissal of his servant at Beersheba, the southernmost limit of Yahweh's land, signifies that he is abandoning [his ministry] altogether."[1] Elijah's reaction to his detour is similar to our own thoughts and reactions when we encounter the unexpected. No wonder the New Testament refers to this prophet as "a man with a nature like ours" (James 5:17).

When life takes us on one of its many detours, we often end up isolated. Sometimes the nature of the detour isolates us. If your detour is a physical infirmity, you may not be able to be around others, or at least not comfortably. Yet most often in the midst of a detour we are alone and isolated at our own choosing. Briefly, let us consider the reasons we isolate ourselves, what the Bible has to say about solitude, the negative effects of isolation, and ways to counteract the tendency toward isolation during a detour.

WHY WE ISOLATE

Why do people on detours isolate themselves? The answers to that question are many, and are as unique as the individuals and the detours themselves. The suggested reasons that follow are not intended as condemnations. They are merely efforts to openly and honestly look at common reasons why we isolate ourselves. Rest assured that isolating oneself is not sin, and periods of withdrawal are not necessarily bad. Much like out-of-control emotions, however, isolation can be dangerous to those on a detour. It is important that we examine our motives in order to discern our purpose for wanting to isolate ourselves.

Embarrassment. When you are on a detour, you feel like you are the only one experiencing what you are experiencing. For example, if you have been laid off, it can be uncomfortable to be around people who are happily and gainfully employed. Even if you did nothing to contribute to your joblessness, the fact that you want a job, you do not have a job, and seemingly everyone else does have a job can be a source of great consternation. Sometimes people just find it easier to be by themselves rather than to be around others and have to endure their own embarrassment at the situation in which they find themselves.

Pain. A detour is a painful experience. Life has gone the wrong direction for you, and being around people whose lives have gone the direction that you anticipated yours going can be very painful. There may be no better illustration of this than those enduring struggles with infertility. They want children, they have been trying to have children, and yet they find themselves on a childless detour. Being around couples who have children or women who are pregnant is painful if infertility is your detour. You would much rather be by yourself than around those who are talking about painting nurseries, choosing cribs, and assembling high chairs.

Feelings of failure. When you are on a detour and life has not gone the way that you planned, often you experience tremendous feelings of failure. Foolishly many view life in terms of success and failure, and so when their life changes course, they feel like failures. People who feel that they have failed typically do not like to admit or dwell on their failures, and being around other people often reinforces those feelings of inadequacy and ineptitude. When you feel like a failure, the last thing that you want is to be surrounded by successful people.

Discouragement. Those on a detour know that their well-meaning friends and family sometimes do not know what to say to be helpful. Words that are meant to encourage can often leave those going through trials feeling emptier than they did before they heard them. Despite the best of intentions, these attempts to uplift can have the opposite effect. People on a detour, weary from all that life has laid in front of them, are often wearied further hearing that everything is going to be okay. It is not that words of encouragement are bad, but for those on a detour, words can be of little comfort. When a person reaches the place where attempts at encouragement only discourage, they can decide that it is better to avoid people, particularly those who attempt to cheer them up or set them on the straight path.

Having no answers. Detours beget questions. Not just from the person on the detour, but from others. Just as with attempts at encouragement, these questions are well-meaning, but if there is one thing that a person on a detour does not have, it is answers. People ask you when you are going to get a job, get those children under control, get well, or resolve that conflict, but you have no answers for their questions. Sometimes it can be easier to avoid people and their questions rather than to proceed with the futile exercise of trying to answer their queries.

The list of motivations to isolate ourselves could go on and on. Further, when someone is isolated it is often due to a combination of factors. Perhaps it would be helpful to see these motivations displayed in the emotions and actions of Elijah.

On Mount Carmel Elijah took his place as the greatest of prophets. The wind and rain obeyed him, fire fell from heaven at his beckoning, and those who opposed him paid with their lives. Yet God allowed a turn of events that Elijah could never have foreseen. Instead of revival overtaking Israel and consuming idol worship, the nation saw Elijah receive a promise of his execution. His desire to isolate himself could have had much to do with embarrassment. How much more embarrassing of a situation can you imagine? Elijah, the man who called down fire, had his head on the chopping block—what tragic irony.

Elijah's anger and frustration with God reinforced his feelings of failure. Had he remained in Israel and not been killed, he constantly would have been asked what God was doing, and Elijah had no answer to that question. On top of that, his servant would have tried to encourage him in the face of these devastating setbacks, and every attempt at encouragement would have reminded Elijah of what had gone wrong. Is it any wonder that Elijah sought solitude and isolation?

THE BIBLE AND SOLITUDE

Everyone can use some time alone. When we speak of isolation we are not speaking of the perfectly normal, healthy, spiritual, and periodic desire for solitude. For our purposes, isolation is when our solitude becomes something more, something unbalanced. If left unchecked, a desire for periodic solitude can turn into habitual isolation. Human beings were never intended to spend long periods of time alone relying solely on themselves.

Two biblical concepts illustrate the theological necessity of maintaining a balance between solitude and relationships. The first concept is found in Genesis 2. In this passage, God has just finished creating, and has given Adam instructions concerning the Tree of Knowledge of Good and Evil. Next God proclaims that it is not good for man, in this case Adam, to be alone (v. 18). This is somewhat strange considering that seven times in Genesis chapter 1 God looked over everything that He created and said it was good. In fact, the last of these seven references to creation being good is in 1:31, where the Scriptures say, "God saw all that He had made, and behold, it was *very* good" (emphasis mine). So it is more than a little surprising to see God proclaim something not good in Genesis 2:18.

The lack of goodness that God sees does not have to do with His creation. As one commentator put it, God "does not find a lack of goodness in anything that has already been created. Rather, the lack of goodness rests in the solitary state of humankind. Humankind needs humankind. We were not created to dwell in isolation, but rather in relationship."[2] God's solution to Adam's loneliness was to create a companion for him, the first woman, Eve. From the beginning the Scriptures teaches us that human beings were not created to be alone.

Given the basic principle that humankind was not created to be alone, we might find it surprising that Jesus, on more than one occasion, sought out solitude. The example of Christ shows us that solitude can be good and useful. In Matthew 4:1–2, Jesus went into the desert alone, led by the Holy Spirit, to be tempted by Satan. He was there by himself for forty days. In Luke 6:12–13, Jesus spent the night alone on a mountain praying to God about the selection of the disciples. In Matthew 14:13, when Jesus heard of the death of John the Baptist, He withdrew by himself in a boat. In Matthew 14:23, Jesus again withdrew by himself to a mountain to pray. Luke 5:16 even tells us that "Jesus Himself would often slip away to the wilderness and pray." Obviously, if Jesus at times sought solitude, it is not a sin. It is important to remember, especially for those on a detour, that there is a difference between periodic solitude and isolation.

Periodic times of solitude are good. These moments of aloneness, like those exhibited by Christ, are relatively short, normally less than twenty-four hours, and characterized by prayer, with a focus on getting to know God in a more intimate way. These times keep us spiritually and mentally clear, sharp, and focused; they contribute to our spiritual and mental health and well being.

Extended periods of time without sincere human interaction are not good. These lengthy times of avoiding people and neglecting to honestly interact with our fellow believers in Christ go beyond brief solitude and stretch into isolation. Instead of being healthy, these prolonged periods of isolation are detrimental to a person's well being. Without others in our life as we go through a detour, our spirit can become defeated and our thinking clouded.

THE HARMFUL EFFECTS OF ISOLATION

The idea that it is not good for humans to be alone is hardly novel. As usual the Word of God was way ahead of the curve, but a host of experts and studies have sounded the alarm too, particularly in our fast-paced and fragmented society. Today more than ever human beings are able to get by with little human interaction. Phone calls, e-mail, Facebook, Twitter, text messaging, and a host of other innovations have replaced face-to-face interaction, even among those who love and care about each other. If people so desired, they could sit on their couches and shop for their groceries on the Internet, bank from their phone, and download a book from the library on an e-reader. Consider these statistics from the General Social Survey:

- A quarter of Americans say they have no one with whom they can discuss personal troubles, more than double the number who were similarly isolated in 1985.
- The number of people Americans have in their closest circle of confidantes has dropped from around three to about two.
- Compared with 1985, nearly 50 percent more people in 2004 reported that their spouse is the only person they can confide in.
- Whereas nearly three-quarters of people in 1985 reported they had a friend in whom they could confide, only half in 2004 said they could count on such support.
- The number of people who said they counted a neighbor as a confidante dropped by more than half, from about 19 percent to about 8 percent.[3]

A *Washington Post* article summarized the problem insightfully: "intimate social ties—once seen as an integral part of daily life and associated with a host of psychological and civic benefits—are shrinking or nonexistent. In bad times, far more people appear to suffer alone."[4]

Though the Bible was the first to declare that isolation was not good, the rest of the world has caught on. Medical professionals, mental health experts, and sociologists all agree that there can be severe consequences when people isolate themselves. As one expert said, "Loneliness . . . can make us less able to get beyond even the normal disruptions, setbacks, and mistakes of day-to-day life. The inability to let go of such events has, in turn, consequences that are not just social but physiological."[5] Consider these negative side effects of isolation.

Isolation is a risk factor for the onset of depression. A 2000 study on the factors leading to depression in later life found that a dominant risk factor was isolation. According to the study, "Having a marital partner, and if unmarried having social support, significantly reduced the impact of functional disabilities on the incidence of depression."[6] Human interaction does not guarantee a resistance to depression, but it can decrease susceptibility to depression, and it can help one deal with many of the effects of depression.

Isolated people are more fatigued. Research by University of Chicago psychologist John Cacioppo has suggested a link between fatigue and isolation. His thesis, tested in a study at The Ohio State University, is that isolation affects people's sleep patterns and thus, solely due to their lack of social connection, lonely people are more fatigued. Cacioppo concluded:

> At Ohio State, when we asked participants to wear a device called the 'nightcap' to record changes in the depth and quality of their sleep, we found that total sleep time did not differ across the groups. However, lonely young adults reported taking longer to fall asleep and also feeling greater daytime fatigue. Our studies of older

adults yielded similar findings, and longitudinal analyses confirmed that it was loneliness specifically that was associated with changes in daytime fatigue. Even though the lonely got the same quantity of sleep as the nonlonely, their quality of sleep was greatly diminished.[7]

Isolation can affect a person's intellectual capabilities. A few years ago at the University of Michigan Institute for Social Research, seventy-six college students were given tests that measured intellectual performance, the speed of mental processing, and how well their memory worked. Before the tests, students were split into three groups. The first group discussed a social issue for ten minutes before they took the tests. The second group completed three tasks, including a crossword puzzle. The third group watched a ten-minute clip of the television sitcom *Seinfeld*. According to one of the researchers, "We found that short-term social interaction lasting for just 10 minutes boosted participants' intellectual performance as much as engaging in so-called 'intellectual' activities for the same amount of time." The researchers concluded that "visiting with a friend or neighbor may be just as helpful in staying sharp as doing a daily crossword puzzle."[8]

Isolation can shorten a life span. A 2010 study conducted by scientists at Brigham Young University and the University of North Carolina found that people with poor social networks, such as those who live alone, have few or no close friends, do not take part in other social activities, or perhaps are unemployed— are twice as likely to die within any given time period, when compared to those who do have a good social network and quality interactions. "This finding remained consistent across age, sex, initial health status, cause of death, and follow-up period."[9]

These results are startling. People who isolate themselves actually have a greater chance of dying than those who maintain normal, healthy relationships, even if they are in the midst of a stressful and emotional detour. Your friends might not be perfect, they might not understand what you are going through, they might even be a pain to deal with, but maintaining those relationships might save your life.

MOVING PAST ISOLATION

In theory, unlike unfulfilled expectations or out-of-control emotions, isolation should be easy to correct: just go find people. However, merely being in the presence of your fellow human beings does not mean you are not isolated. A person could be constantly surrounded by people and still feel isolated. With that in mind, here are five things to consider to overcome isolation.

Rely on God's Truth

Earlier in this chapter we discussed a few reasons why people isolate themselves when they are in the midst of a detour. Whether our reason is disappointment, anger, or embarrassment, the emotion leaves us feeling like we are the only one who has ever been on this particular detour before. If it is your child who is having behavioral issues, your marriage that is on the rocks, or your health that is poor, we can quickly believe that we should isolate ourselves because no one has ever had this problem before, or at least no one has had this problem as severely as we have. In order to move on we will need to focus on relying on God's revealed truth.

While the desire to isolate is certainly a valid emotion, and one we need to deal with, we must realize that our shame at being on a detour has more to do with believing Satan's lies about us than living a life of faith. On a detour we isolate because our problems seem so large, and we feel that in some way we must have caused them. The truth, however, is that God knew the detour was coming, allowed it to come, and is there with us on the detour, even if we do not feel His presence like we wish we did. Yet, God promises that as His children, nothing can separate us from Him (Romans 8:31–39). When we feel the urge to isolate ourselves, we must intentionally rely on what God says in His Word.

Pray

Why is it so hard to pray in the midst of a detour? For some the difficulty in praying during a detour has to do with frustration and anger with God. For others it has to do with boredom and monotony, the feeling like you are uttering the same prayers constantly. For still others there is the desire to see God work before again exercising faith in prayer. For all of these reasons and more, despite the fact that prayer has never been more important, it will rarely be more difficult than when you are on a detour. Because of this difficulty, three practices follow that will help you focus your prayer life during a detour.

First, on a detour you must remember to pray regularly. The temptation to shorten or even totally ignore your prayer time in favor of more "productive" pursuits is intense when life has taken an unexpected turn. However, if you do not make prayer intentional, it will not happen. A prayer time that is expendable is a prayer time that will be neglected.

Second, on a detour you must remember to pray for others, not just yourself. One of the side effects of detours is that they can make you see life as if you were wearing blinders. Before long you are able to see only your own problems. While you do need to pray for yourself and the situation you are in, intentionally praying for others while on your detour will help you to maintain perspective and remember that there is a world outside of you and your problems.

Third, on a detour you must remember to pray honestly. It is a quirk of human nature that we seem to struggle to be honest with God when God already knows our thoughts, but often this is the case. Praying false and disingenuous prayers will only weaken your prayer life. While we may fear that God will not appreciate our honesty, we must remember that He already knows our thoughts and feelings. Honesty is required for us, not for Him.

Avoid Feeling Sorry for Yourself

While my wife and I were on one of our recent detours, she was talking to a dear friend of hers about our struggles, and her friend's advice, after listening and empathizing with our situation, was for my wife to, "Put on your big girl panties and deal with it." That advice may be blunt, but it conveys a good message. We need to express and be honest about our frustrations, but we cannot continue to dwell on them and feel sorry for ourselves and our plight.

To survive a detour you will need other people. To interact with other people you will need to put aside your pride, and realize that the world still keeps turning despite what is going on in your life. Examine how you are reacting to your detour, and see if you are willing to think and live outside of your comfort zone to deal with your unexpected circumstances. Avoid the urge to feel sorry for yourself.

Get Connected

Part of the reason why isolation comes so easily in the midst of a detour is that many of us are not incredibly well connected with other people to begin with. In our world, face-to-face interaction has been so minimized that we have to be intentional about developing relationships. If you have quality relationships, then a detour is the time to invest in them, not to isolate from them. If you do not have quality relationships, then there is no time like the present to begin building them.

Your church, your family, and a host of other options can help you get connected to other people. Find people who share your faith and are willing to put in the time and effort to grow a genuine friendship. You may not come by those people easily, but often we "do not have because [we] do not ask" (James 4:2). Often we do not have quality friends because we do not put forth the effort to be quality friends, and to develop good relationships. Realize that quality relationships with the people of God are not a luxury, they are a necessity, and with that in mind do not stop pursuing them until you have reached your objective. Let Matthew 7:7–12 be your focus in seeking relationships:

> *Ask, and it will be given to you; seek, and you will find; knock, and it will be opened to you. For everyone who asks receives, and he who seeks finds, and to him who knocks it will be opened. Or what man is there among you who, when his son asks for a loaf, will give him a stone? Or if he asks for a fish, he will not give him a snake, will he? If you then,*

being evil, know how to give good gifts to your children, how much more will your Father who is in heaven give what is good to those who ask Him! In everything, therefore, treat people the same way you want them to treat you, for this is the Law and the Prophets.

Get Real

Some people do not have many relationships, and others have tons of relationships, none of which are very deep. Overcoming the tendency to isolate is not merely having friends who will discuss the latest TV shows with you. The kind of relationships that will aid you in your detour are honest and sincere. These types of friends will be willing to listen to your frustrations and anger, but they will also encourage you to move past the desire to isolate yourself. These are also the toughest relationships to develop. Much like the pot of gold at the end of a rainbow, they are often what everyone wants, but no one can seem to find.

The easiest test of a relationship's authenticity is to share with your friend your anger and frustration with God. Everyone gets angry with God at times. Think of the powerful emotions that Elijah experienced. Those emotions were not pretty, and they caused him to head to the wilderness. The ability to express our angst with a God who is all-powerful, but whose plan for us seems to have come unhinged, is one of the most elemental pieces of a good friendship. You know you have a quality friendship when you say, "I am angry at God," and your friend says, "Me too. Let's talk about that."

Superficiality so often rules the day with friendships because it is safe and comfortable, but those on a detour cannot afford to simply be safe and comfortable. You feel like your life is careening out of control and you need a friend. You might reveal yourself to someone who proves to be a bad friend, and in fact there is a good chance of that happening. However, if you do not bring authenticity to a relationship, you will never find authentic friends.

My loneliness in Amsterdam did not last long. I had just enough local currency to buy another train ticket, and since I knew the hotel we were staying at, I was able to ask for directions. When I arrived at the correct train station, everyone was there waiting for me. My detour and my loneliness were over. Your detour, and the loneliness that can accompany it, may not be overcome by the simple purchase of a train ticket. However, allowing yourself to become isolated will only make your detour more difficult. Maintaining quality friendships will not solve all of your problems, but it may mean the difference between being stranded on a detour and surviving a detour.

QUESTIONS FOR DISCUSSION

1. How many close friends do you have? Can you truly count on them when you are in a detour?
2. What can you do to be more purposeful about developing quality friendships?
3. Do you struggle with loneliness during detours?
4. What are some specific steps that you can take to prevent your isolation?

FOUR

DETOURS AND COMPARISON

1 Kings 19:4

Comparison.

The word comes out of your mouth with a thud. Maybe for you it brings to mind the time in high school when you tried to race your peers in a hurdles event and discovered as your face was swiftly plummeting toward the track that that would not be your finest hour (and that was just the first hurdle). Maybe it makes you recall that time you were passed over for a raise or promotion. Maybe it reminds you of that actor or actress who looks like you want to look.

Our society not only embraces comparison, it feasts on it like a hungry crocodile feeds on an unsuspecting zebra. You can go online to compare cameras or other gizmos that you want to buy. You can sort your comparison by price, function, specifications, or even the ratings of other consumers. You can compare airplane ticket and hotel prices at an almost endless number of travel websites. You can compare health plans, neighborhoods, restaurants, doctors, hospitals, cars, jobs, churches, and even other people, if you so choose.

The Internet has taken our natural bent toward comparison and developed it into an art form. With just a click you can:

- Compare how much you look like Kenny Rogers at MenWhoLookLikeKennyRogers.com. Based on this website I look nothing like Kenny Rogers. Judge for yourself how good or bad that is.
- Make yourself feel better about your family by examining the strangeness of other families at AwkwardFamilyPhotos.com. My family, at least my immediate family, looks downright normal compared to most of those photos.
- Compare your writing style to that of famous writers at the *I Write Like* website http://iwl.me. According to that website, the writing in the first chapter of this book is similar to that of Dan Brown, author of *The DaVinci Code.* Hopefully my book is a little less heretical and better researched.
- Compare your cost of living at BestPlaces.net/col. Were my wife and I to decide to move from Little Elm, Texas, to Sheboygan, Wisconsin, the cost of living there is slightly lower. It is way too cold in Wisconsin for me to ever leave the house, but it is nice to know we could make it in Sheboygan if the need arose.

Perhaps there is no greater forum for comparison than the little slice of purgatory we call high school, or maybe that was just my experience. The brand of your clothes, the color of your sneakers, the cut of your hair, the car you drove, what you watched on television, who you spent your time with, whether or not you played sports, and an almost infinite number of other factors were used to compare one another, and God help you if you did not measure up.

Unfortunately, the comparisons do not stop when we graduate high school, do they? After high school you enter college, where you encounter even more comparisons, and these seem to have more riding on them than those in high school. In college if you do not compare favorably, then you are not just uncool, you are uncool and probably can't get a job or a mate either. Then after college you get married, start a career, and have children, but the comparisons keep coming. How your baked chicken compares to your mother-in-law's, how thorough your reports are compared to your coworkers' reports, and how well behaved your children are next to your friends' kids at church are just a few of the many comparisons with which we find ourselves struggling. Then one day you are older and comparing retirement plans, grandchildren's pictures, false teeth, and knee replacements.

The comparisons never stop. As we will see from our friend Elijah, the temptation and desire to compare is ever present, particularly to the person on a detour. In verse 4 of 1 Kings 19 we see the continuation of Elijah's detour:

> But he himself went a day's journey into the wilderness, and came and sat down under a juniper tree; and he requested for himself that he might die, and said, "It is enough; now, O Lord, take my life, for I am not better than my fathers."

Two things in particular are interesting about Elijah in this verse.

First, take note of the prophet's actions. Beersheba, where Elijah left his servant and continued on alone, was the most southern point of the land of Judah. Although the territory of

Judah actually extended some sixty miles farther south, Beer-sheba was the end of cultivated land and population. Elijah left the northern kingdom of Israel, passed through the southern kingdom of Judah, and then kept going another day's journey. This action is very curious, and has troubled readers of the passage. Why did Elijah run so far? One commentator suggests, "A day's journey . . . is as far as he intends to go; he lies down weary unto death and prays for Yahweh to let it be enough; his forefathers are in their graves, let him be as they are, for he is no better than they."[1] By removing himself from his homeland and the land of his ministry, Elijah was most likely indicating that as far as he was concerned his life and his ministry were over.

Second, take note of Elijah's words. If you thought the powerful prophet was acting strange—and you would not be alone in that assessment—then his words only further confuse you about this once mighty prophet. More than a few scholars, pastors, and students of the Bible have weighed in on these incredibly negative words that come from lips which only days before had called down fire from heaven. Dr. Howard Hendricks suggests that these words are the ultimate in hypocrisy:

> The longer I examine this, the more I think there is a touch of the hypocritical in Elijah's prayer. I don't think Elijah wanted to die. If he had wanted to die, he did not have to travel 120 miles south. All he had to do was to make himself available to Jezebel. She'd be delighted to accommodate him. Have you ever thanked God for the blessings of unanswered prayer? I sometimes think of the moronic things I have asked God for and I'm so glad He never answered them the way I expected. Prayer is not asking for what you want; it is asking for what He wants.[2]

No doubt there is more than a tinge of hypocrisy in Elijah's words. Where there had once been bravery and boldness we now see disappointment and exasperation. The man who had urged Israel to abandon the impotent Baal and to serve the powerful God of Israel had fled his people at the time of their greatest need.

At the root of Elijah's words is not just hypocrisy, it is something more—a comparison in which he falls short. Elijah says, "I am not better than my fathers" (v. 4). The "fathers" that Elijah mentions could refer to his earthly ancestors, but more than likely he is referring to the prophets that had ministered before him, his spiritual ancestors. Prior to the life of Elijah, many prophets had ministered to the united kingdom of Israel, and later to the southern kingdom of Judah and northern kingdom of Israel after the nation split. All of these prophets, though experiencing varied degrees of success, had ultimately been unable to stop Israel's and Judah's slides into sin. Now Elijah sees his name being added to that list.

Elijah was intelligent enough to realize that the real spiritual problem in Israel lay with its leadership. He had hoped that the great miracles that God had worked through him would be enough to finally stem the tide of wickedness that had flooded over Israel's leaders. The death threat from Jezebel told him that a three-year drought, hundreds of slain prophets of Baal, and fire from heaven had only hardened the hearts of Israel's royalty. Elijah saw himself as failing where those before him had failed. He sits down under a juniper tree, compares himself to his predecessors, and concludes his life and ministry were failures. This failure is more than he can bear, and so he asks God to kill him. Elijah has decided that death is preferable for him. He has been no more successful trying to bring about repentance in Israel than any other prophet before him. In fact, he believes that he has only momentarily slowed the nation's inevitable decline. Rather than sticking around for Jezebel to victoriously chop off his head, he went as far south as he could go, where at least if he died the wicked queen would not receive credit. The prophet is broken, and he is fatalistic about his fate and that of his people.

Asking for God to kill you is a drastic measure for sure, but not an entirely unexpected one given Elijah's mind-set. In his mind he is an abject failure. When he compares himself to his predecessors, he has had no more success than they have, and when he compares what happened to what he wanted to happen, he sees his life as a total waste. Rather than dying at the hand of the vile Queen of Israel, he at least hopes that God will have mercy on him and kill him himself.

We have seen Elijah's expectations go unmet, which led to emotions that were out of control. Those emotions then pushed Elijah to isolate himself. And now we see Elijah, emotional and isolated, fall victim to one of the greatest traps inherit to humanity—the trap of comparison. Let's look at what scientific research has discovered about humans and comparison, examine the flaws of comparison, and then use what the Scriptures tell us about comparison to come to a position on comparison informed by God's Word—a position that will help us when we are on a detour.

HUMAN NATURE AND COMPARISON

Much as with emotions and isolation, modern science has done a fantastic job of confirming what we will see that the Bible revealed thousands of years ago. That human beings compare themselves to one another almost obsessively seems obvious when you even casually observe our culture, and probably reflect on your own actions. However, the skeptics can consider these two revealing studies.

A few years ago Joanne Wood and her colleagues at the University of Waterloo performed an experiment in which participants were given a series of tests. After the tests were completed, some of the participants were told that they had performed well on the tests and some were told that they had failed. Next the participants were tasked with selecting a test for an unseen partner in a separate room. The participants who had been told that they had done poorly almost always assigned their unseen partner the most challenging test possible.[3] Apparently when people fail, they want everyone else to fail as well.

Another study, conducted several years ago, concluded that people are concerned with comparing their financial status with others. In the study, people were given the choice of living in a world in which they receive an annual salary of $50,000 when others receive an annual salary of $25,000, or living in a world where they receive an annual salary of $100,000 when everyone else receives an annual salary of $200,000. Any guess which one people chose? Overwhelmingly, people chose to make less money and live in a world in which their salary was lower but higher than everyone else's. As one psychologist said of the study,

> Research in psychology and economics suggests that when only *your* salary is cut, you make a foolish investment, or you lose your job, you become considerably less satisfied with your life. But when *everyone* becomes worse off, your life satisfaction remains pretty much the same. We care more about social comparison, about status, about rank, and about so-called positional goods than about the absolute value of our bank accounts or reputations.[4]

What this study revealed was that while almost everyone wishes they made more money, people are not nearly as concerned with how much they make as they are with how much they make compared to everyone else. We all want to make more money, but the study reveals that we want to make more than our fellow employees, not more per paycheck. Human beings are hardwired to compare themselves with one another.

Today, psychologists characterize social comparison in two ways: upward and downward. In upward comparison, people compare themselves to someone who is considered to be above them in some way. By comparing themselves to this person, they make themselves seem better or an equal. In downward comparison, people compare themselves to someone who is considered inferior; this comparison makes them feel better about themselves because they seem superior.

Human beings are definitely emotional beings. They are definitely social beings. And they are most definitely comparative beings, but is all of that comparison actually beneficial?

THE FLAWS OF COMPARISON

Some people are more inclined to compare themselves than others. Take my wife and me, for example. I am an only child who did not grow up comparing myself to siblings. My wife, on the other hand, is the middle child. Like most middle children she has spent much of her life evaluating herself in relation to her older brother and her younger sister. My family values independence to a fault, so much so that if my maternal grandfather (who was known to have a less than firm grasp of history) was to be believed, I am descended from a signer of the United States Declaration of Independence and a signer of the Texas Declaration of Independence. Pretty much if someone was declaring their independence we wanted in on it. While my wife and I both struggle with comparisons at times, overcoming the tendency to compare comes much easier to me because of family dynamics and my personality.

Not all comparisons are bad. Comparing our talents, abilities, and skills against others can be healthy and beneficial, but using comparison to determine our value or worth as a person is both foolish and dangerous. From the time that I was in kindergarten through my graduation from high school, my father was either one of my teachers or the principal. Because he was the principal for most of those years, he (and consequently his son who rode with him) would get to school well before everyone else, including other teachers. Since we were both there so early we would often go to the gymnasium and play table tennis together. The first time that we ever played table tennis my dad beat me rather mercilessly. Then he beat me every time that we played. I would ask my loving father to let me win, but he would tell me that one day I would beat him on my own, and when I did it would be because I was better, not because he let me win. This might have caused another child to give up, but my dad knew that because of my competitive nature it would only make me better. Years passed and then one day I beat my dad at table tennis. All those years of losing, of comparing my skills to my dad's skills, had improved my game to the point that I was very good. He has steadfastly refused to play me in table tennis ever since because now he does not like the comparison.

Tests, games, scores, report cards, and competitions all have their place. They are measures for discovering what needs improvement. As with emotion, in and of themselves none of these tools are bad, but they can quickly become a hindrance. When students take a history test and one of the students cannot remember that Abraham Lincoln was the sixteenth president of the United States, it reveals only that the student answered a question incorrectly that other students answered correctly. The missed question might indicate a number of things. It might reveal that the student has bad study habits, poor memory techniques, or a learning disability. Maybe the student does not like history, is unmotivated, or is having trouble at home. What it most definitely does not reveal is that the particular student is somehow inferior or less valuable than other students; the student merely needs to learn more about history. Unfortunately, when we compare ourselves, all too often we do not simply evaluate skills or abilities but make value judgments about our worth as a person relative to others. Because of this, more often than not, comparison is not only counterproductive, it is just plain foolish.

For a moment ponder three flaws in our attempts to compare ourselves to others.

Comparison Has a Timing Problem

On April 13, 1954, the Milwaukee Braves and the Cincinnati Redlegs met in the first baseball game of the major league season. That day each team started a young player in left field. The Reds' leftfielder was twenty-six–year-old Jim Greengrass. Greengrass was starting his third season in the major leagues, and through his first two seasons he had shown a lot of promise. That day against the Braves, Greengrass had four hits in five at bats and scored two runs. He was well on his way to fulfilling his promise. The player for the Braves that day was an inexperienced rookie who was just past his twentieth birthday. He came to the plate five times and failed to get one hit. Though people expected a lot from this rookie, he showed little talent and ability that first game. Yet despite a rough start, Hank Aaron went on to a successful career. By 1957 Greengrass was out of baseball, and Hank Aaron had hit 66 of his career 755 homeruns.

One of the biggest problems of comparison is that of timing. Comparing Jim Greengrass to Hank Aaron after the first game of the 1954 baseball season would have told you little about each player. The one who played poorly that day went on to become one of greatest players in the game. Comparing ourselves is often like comparing Greengrass and Aaron after opening day. We tend to focus on the immediate time in comparison while ignoring the past and forgetting that we have a future that is still unknown.

Comparison Has Partial Truth Problem

When you get right down to it, we do not know enough about others to compare ourselves. We get all worked up because in the midst of a detour life seems a lot tougher for us than it does for others. God has allowed our circumstances to spin out of control, but everyone else seems to have things so easy. Our health is bad, our families are in chaos, our finances are in the tank, and we seem to be the only one with these problems. The flaw in this thinking is that we base our comparison upon partial truths. We have no idea what other people's lives are truly like.

All human beings are trained actors. Most of us do an Academy Award–worthy job of pretending like our lives are perfect and that we have no serious problems. Therefore, when we compare ourselves to others, we base our comparison on bad information. Imagine that you are searching real estate listings for a new home. What you don't know is that in the neighborhood in which you want to move, all of the homes listed bear no resemblance to their descriptions. Instead of listing their homes as simple three- and four- bedroom houses, every homeowner in the neighborhood claims their house is a million-dollar mansion. Based on the listing information, a simple three-bedroom, two-bath home would seem incredibly inferior to the surrounding houses. In reality our lives are all fixer-upper projects pretending to be million-dollar homes. How could you possibly use that as a comparison?

Comparison Has a Pride Problem

When we compare ourselves to other people our motivation is rarely pure. As C. S. Lewis once said, "Pride gets no pleasure out of having something, only out of having more of it than the next man . . . It is the comparison that makes you proud: the pleasure of being above the rest."[5] Lewis's words are most definitely true in light of the results of a Gallup poll in August 2010.[6] That poll found that as the economy got worse, people became happier with their wages. In August of 2008, with the U.S. unemployment rate at 6.1 percent, 51 percent of people surveyed felt that they were underpaid. However, in August of 2010, with the U.S. unemployment rate at 9.6 percent only 43 percent of people felt that they were underpaid.

While unemployment rose steadily over those two years, people's satisfaction with their pay increased. As Marina Krakovsky hypothesized about the study in an issue of *Psychology Today*,

> People have a well-established tendency to judge their material well-being in relation to others—even after taking buying power into account. Some of the satisfied workers may not have been earning as much as they had

the year before, but we would bet many were happy to just have a job at all—all the more so after seeing rising unemployment numbers, stories of people losing their homes, and perhaps layoffs at their own workplace. We're social creatures, and just hearing and seeing the misfortune of others can make many of us feel we're coming out ahead.[7]

Even in difficult times people have a tendency to be concerned with how they compare to others. Pride pushes us to compare ourselves, and to conclude that we are better than others.

THE BIBLE AND COMPARISON

So far we have seen comparison is a part of human nature, and it is as flawed as it is natural. Now comes the most important part of considering comparison: What does the Bible tell us about comparison?

Human Beings Are Poor Objects of Comparison

In 2 Corinthians chapter 10 the apostle Paul defends himself against those who challenged his authority as an apostle. These challengers found the apostle to be unimpressive and less than they expected in person saying, "His letters are weighty and strong, but his personal presence is unimpressive and his speech contemptible" (2 Corinthians 10:10). Evidently those who were urging rebellion against Paul's authority felt that they themselves were much more forceful and effective in person. This attitude was countered by Paul. The apostle wrote, "Oh, don't worry; [I] wouldn't dare say that [I am] as wonderful as these other men who tell you how important they are! But they are only comparing themselves with each other, using themselves as the standard of measurement. How ignorant!" (2 Corinthians 10:12 NLT).

The opposition to the apostle went about comparison by setting themselves up as the measuring stick by which they evaluated themselves and others. In the first century, when Paul wrote the letter to the Corinthians, comparison was used as a common technique by orators and philosophers. Yet Paul's opponents were not using this technique properly. One scholar writes, "Here Paul mocks his opponents: they are so foolish that they do not realize that one cannot compare oneself with oneself."[8]

It was also common for a person of a higher social class to write a letter of recommendation for someone who was socially inferior. There were times, however, that a person was so destitute and without friends of a higher class that he would have to discreetly write his own commendation. For someone to openly commend himself was considered highly pretentious, a vice in Greek culture.[9] In 2 Corinthians, Paul points out that his opponents are foolish both in their comparisons and how they went about them.

The irony of all of this is that despite all of their self-promotion, they showed by comparing themselves to each other that they lacked the ability to properly perceive and understand the spiritual life. Like a boy playing himself in a board game, they were assured of coming out on top.

Christ Is the Only Viable Object of Comparison

Thank God for the Corinthian church and its problems. If it was not for their issues we would miss valuable pieces of God's revelation. In 2 Corinthians we learned that people make poor objects of comparison, and in 1 Corinthians we learn the only accurate measuring stick is Jesus Christ himself. The Corinthians had a bad habit of comparing, even of comparing the people that they followed. Some claimed that Paul was superior, some claimed that Peter was superior, and on and on the comparisons went.

Frustrated by their constant need to choose sides and pick teams, the apostle Paul told this most dysfunctional of churches, "Be imitators of me, just as I also am of Christ" (1 Corinthians 11:1). The Greek word that our English Bibles translate as "imitate" is *mimetes*. *Mimetes* was a word used to describe actors or impersonators, and it is also the origin of the modern term "mimic." The only comparison that is valid for Christians is that of comparing themselves to Christ. If we compare ourselves to another person, it is only to be in the context of how that person impersonates Christ. As C. S. Lewis once said, "In God you come up against something which is in every respect immeasurably superior to yourself. Unless you know God as that—and, therefore, know yourself as nothing in comparison—you do not know God at all."[10]

Comparison Neglects Eternity

By its very nature, comparison is focused on the here and now, for it is hard to compare the future because you do not know what the future holds. Even Jesus' own handpicked disciples struggled with comparison, and He pointed out that they could not make an accurate assessment because they did not know the future. After his resurrection, Jesus and His disciples were together and Jesus prophesied that Peter would die as a martyr (John 21:18–19). Peter responded to this shocking revelation by asking what would become of the disciple John. Jesus responded to Peter's attempt at comparing his future with John's by telling the curious disciple, "If I want him to remain until I come, what is that to you? You follow Me" (v. 22).

As believers in Christ, many of our comparisons are often rooted in what we feel is God's unfairness as our Father. On a detour your brain may tell you that God is a loving God, but your heart tells you that God is allowing you to undergo hardships while other children of His sail through life with nary a storm. Our comparisons, however, fail to consider eternity. While it may appear that God is unfair to us with relation to others, we make our comparisons neglecting to consider that our life here on earth is only the first act.

Whenever we compare, we never measure up, and the resulting feelings of inadequacy do not go away. They remain, even if below the surface, where they continually simmer. If we do not deal with our comparison problem, at some point feelings about our perceived shortfalls will begin to boil over, causing more and more problems for us on our detours. This can lead to neglecting to take care of fundamentals that can be quite costly when ignored.

QUESTIONS FOR DISCUSSION

1. How strong is the temptation to compare for you?
2. Do you struggle with comparing yourself to a person or a particular group?
3. What does the desire to compare tell us about ourselves?
4. How does knowing that Christ is to be the object of our comparison impact how you think about yourself and others?

FIVE

DETOURS AND TAKING CARE OF YOURSELF

1 Kings 19:5-7

The most wonderful thing about a happy childhood is the absolute lack of stress and worry. While children, particularly those enduring rough circumstances, do experience stress and its effects, many of us grew up blissfully ignorant of the difficulties that our parents and our families were facing. My family did not have a lot in the way of money or worldly possessions, but I was never worried about paying the bills. My parents, and particularly my dad, no doubt carried that burden constantly, but I had no idea that finances were tight. I loved and trusted my parents, and they always fed me so I got up and watched cartoons every Saturday morning never considering what it cost to buy the pancakes I ate for breakfast. My parents, however, probably had a different perspective on those pancakes. They trusted God to take care of us, and He always did, but that does not mean that they did not have some nights where sleep was chased away by the worries and cares of everyday life.

I was thankfully oblivious to all of these stresses and concerns. Whereas people undergoing severe stresses often struggle to eat and sleep, as a child those were the only two things that you could count on me doing consistently. My ability to sleep is so pronounced that it is all but legendary in my family. Numerous times I slept through a near natural disaster, or a moment in which everyone was sure we were doomed. One year for our family vacation my parents and I hitched up the pop-up camper, loaded in the car, and left for Albuquerque, New Mexico. As anyone who has ever lived or visited that part of New Mexico can attest, it can get quite windy. A little wind was not about to derail our vacation, although my dad's inability to find the zoo almost did (more on this later).

One morning I woke up and realized that something must have happened during the night. I had, as usual, slept through the night without so much as turning over, but my parents seemed like they had a rougher time of it. My dad's receding hairline seemed to have entered a full retreat overnight, and my mom looked as if she had been fighting for her life. What I soon found out was that night, while I was fast asleep, incredibly powerful winds had swept through the campground. Entire tents, even some that were occupied, had blown over and been sent rolling down hills. Gusts of wind had blown over trees and power lines, and our little pop-up camper had been tossed to and fro for several hours during the night. This situation had been pretty scary, at least for those that were awake for it; I, however, slept through it like a baby.

Twenty-five years later I found myself in another tense situation, but this time my reaction was far different. I was employed at a job with impossible expectations. I worked as hard and as smart as I could, but I knew that it was not going to be enough. The job's unreasonable demands, my bosses' unwillingness to consider any changes, the pitiful state of the economy, and the company's track record with how it treated its employees all convinced me that I could and probably would be fired at any moment. My wife and I had been trying to get pregnant for a few months without success, and we were also trying to dig ourselves out of a financial hole from an earlier round of layoffs.

Needless to say, my reaction to this situation was far different from the windstorm in Albuquerque. Now instead of sleeping through the night I found myself unable to fall asleep, or waking up and staying awake for hours in the middle of the night. Instead of being happy-go-lucky, I was worried about finding a new job, if there was a problem with us getting pregnant, and how we would be able to pay our bills or get out of debt without my paycheck. I had never been one to lose sleep, as my Albuquerque experience attested, but now I could not seem to get my mind to turn off so that I could get some rest.

In tough and stressful times some people lose not only sleep, but also their appetites. My appetite went the other direction. Instead of missing meals I ate more and more unhealthy food. I would go to work and by lunchtime I was starving and wanting to eat something that tasted good, even if it was not good for me. Instead of a healthy lunch, more often than not I dined on double cheeseburgers, french fries, and a large soft drink from the drive-through of a fast food restaurant. I figured if I was liable to be fired at any moment, my taste buds might as well be happy.

That particular detour was tough on me physically. I was gaining weight, losing sleep, and not taking care of myself. The worst part was that I could see no end in sight. I knew that if I could not find another job, I would be laid off no matter what I did, and so my detour of a bad job only promised to end with another detour of unemployment. Despite my best efforts I seemed to be powerless to do anything but eat, lose sleep, and worry.

Our journey with Elijah continues with him struggling. He has asked God to take his life, and so after a long journey he lies down and anticipates his fate. Verses 5–7 of 1 Kings 19 are as full of surprises as the rest of the chapter:

> He lay down and slept under a juniper tree; and behold, there was an angel touching him, and he said to him, "Arise, eat." Then he looked and behold, there was at his head a bread cake baked on hot stones, and a jar of water. So he ate and drank and lay down again. The angel of the Lord came again a second time and touched him and said, "Arise, eat, because the journey is too great for you."

Elijah's wilderness adventure began with the mighty prophet, fresh off an amazing victory over idolatry, running for his life. He abandoned his country, his servant, and his role as a prophet. Then he declared himself to be a failure and asked God to take his life. Verse 5 finds Elijah waiting for God's response to his demand. For the first time since the beginning of 1 Kings 18, we see him being something he has not been—still. Elijah has requested to die, and now far away from the idolatry of Israel, the wickedness of Ahab and Jezebel, and reminders of his "failure," he simply lies down and goes to sleep.

Stop for a moment and guess what comes next. If you have read this story of Elijah before, try to put that out of your mind and take a fresh look at this experience. God is going to respond to Elijah in some way. What would you expect? Personally, I would expect rebuke, rejection, judgment, maybe another fireball from heaven. Elijah was the most notable of all of God's prophets and he ran away, quit the ministry, and asked to die. At the very least you would expect a whale (or large fish) to appear out of nowhere and swallow Elijah for three days until he straightened up.

Yet God does none of those things. While Elijah is asleep, waiting on God to take His life, he is awoken, not by God's impending judgment, but by an angelic chef. Not an angel with a flaming sword, but instead one who has delivered takeout. A cake of bread and a jug of water await the apparently exhausted prophet. F. B. Meyer writes of this moment,

> God did more than love him. He sought, by tender helpfulness, to heal and restore His servant's soul to its former health and joy. At His command, an angel, twice over, prepared a meal upon the desert sand and touched him and bade him eat. No upbraiding speeches, no word of reproach, no threats of dismissal, but only sleep and food and kindly thoughtfulness.[1]

Elijah's response is almost as curious as God's. He expected God to zap him for his actions, but rather God sent him a to-go meal from heaven's drive-through. Elijah could have concluded that he had been given a second chance; God has provided him food and water for his return to Israel. Instead, when awoken by an angel providing a hot meal, Elijah does not get up from his nap and return to Israel—he goes back to sleep.

Despite the fact that the apparently tired prophet has hit the snooze button, God's angelic messenger is not deterred. He returns to the sleeping seer and again wakes him up to another heaven-cooked meal. The reason that he must once again arise and eat is given by the angel: "Because the journey is too great for you" (v. 7). It is interesting that the Hebrew word used for journey is *derek*. Much like our English term "journey," *derek* is used of both literal and metaphorical journeys. You might speak of your journey to your hometown for the holidays, and you might also speak of your journey through cancer. Though we will see in verse 8 that Elijah has a quite literal journey ahead of him, it is significant to note that another journey is going on as well.

Elijah's detour is similar to ours in that it is happening in two different dimensions simultaneously. There is the earthly dimension in which Elijah's life has been threatened, he has fled Israel, and he has asked to die. But there is also a spiritual dimension in which Elijah has been frustrated, disappointed, and scared. It is in the dimension that eyes cannot see where the battle for Elijah's future as a prophet was taking place. In the next few chapters we will see how Elijah's spiritual journey will become clearer, but before we get there let's spend some time looking at the physical journey of someone on a detour.

THE DETOUR SPIRAL

People on a detour spend a great deal of time trying to find a way around the detour. If you live anywhere that has road construction, you have no doubt experienced the sinking feeling of getting stuck in the resulting traffic. As soon as I realize that the cars in front of me are not moving and that I will not be going anywhere anytime soon, I begin to try to find an alternate route. First, I rack my brain for side streets, parallel roads, shortcuts—anything I can think of to get around the backup of vehicles. If that does not work, then I pull out my phone and punch up the map to see if there is a way around the construction site.

People on a detour function much like I do in traffic. They think, they plan, they scheme, they work, they cajole, they push, they pull, they do anything that they can to end their detour, but the work and planning usually serve to only further the frustrated feelings of the detour. All of your effort to get out of the detour just makes it worse. Before long a detour can begin to take the shape of a downward spiral. Your experience may resemble that of Elijah's. You had to deal with unmet expectations, which led to unbalanced emotions, which in turn led you to isolate yourself, which had you comparing yourself to others. Along the way you were probably trying to think and work your way out of the detour. The process may have felt like this:

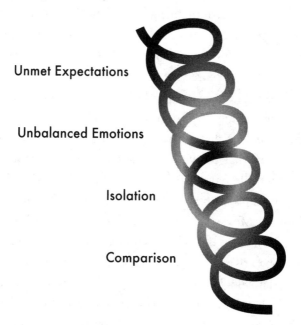

Unmet Expectations

Unbalanced Emotions

Isolation

Comparison

The problem is that your mighty efforts to rid yourself of a detour end up being more like quicksand than stepping stone. In an October 2008 episode of the Discovery Channel's *Man vs. Wild*, adventurer Bear Grylls finds himself stuck in quicksand in the Moab Desert in Utah. Slowly he begins to sink in the mixture of sand and water, and the more he struggles against the quicksand, the deeper he sinks. Eventually he manages to free himself, but only after he stops struggling against the quicksand that has imprisoned him.

Our detours can often be like quicksand. You hope to emerge from your troubles, but the more you try to get out of them, the more you seem to become engulfed in them. The more you struggle and the more you fight, the more despairing your detour can become. Instead of finding yourself breaking free, you are instead spiraling down further and further. Your attempts to rid yourself of the detour only seem to increase your unmet expectations, make your emotions more unbalanced, push you to be more isolated, and cause you to compare yourself to even more people who seem to be having the time of their lives while you are slogging through the depths of despair.

The trouble is that we have grown up in a culture that has stressed to us that the way to overcome problems is to defeat them. When life hands you lemons, you make lemonade, and then you put up a lemonade stand, sell the lemonade, and become a millionaire. Movies and television have shown us that if life hits you, you hit it back. If you lose your job, you just keep looking for another job until you find one. You send resumes, make contacts, go to job fairs, look at job boards, and refuse to take no for an answer. If that does not work, you do it all over again, only you do it more and better until eventually you get a new job.

If you want to avoid cancer, you eat certain foods, avoid other foods, hit the gym often, avoid unhealthy activities like smoking, and get regular checkups. You do all of that, and then somehow you still get cancer. So then you do it all bigger and better because that is how you keep cancer from coming back. You work harder and smarter than everyone else because that is the way to success and overcoming obstacles—or at least that is what we have been told.

We have been trained to approach detours like Teddy Roosevelt did getting shot. Roosevelt left the United States presidency in 1909 after two terms, but by the end of 1911 he had decided that he wanted to occupy the Oval Office once again. Instead of running as a Republican as he had before, he ran under the banner of the Progressive Party. Roosevelt campaigned tirelessly and with just three weeks to go until the election, he set out on a last campaign trip. October 14 found the former president campaigning in Milwaukee, Wisconsin. As he made his way from his hotel room to the auditorium where he would give his campaign speech, Roosevelt was approached by John F. Schrank, a saloon-keeper from New York. Schrank pulled a gun and shot Roosevelt at close range with a .38 caliber revolver. The bullet passed through a metal case that held his reading glasses and Roosevelt's fifty–page speech, which had been folded over several times to fit in his pocket. The case and the speech had slowed the bullet significantly, but it still lodged in his chest.

Roosevelt did not think that the wound was fatal, but the doctors who examined him ordered that he be taken to a hospital. Roosevelt would have none of it. With some difficulty he made his way to the podium and said, "Friends, I shall ask you to be as quiet as possible. I don't know whether you fully understand that I have just been shot; but it takes more than that to kill a Bull Moose . . . The bullet is in me now, so that I cannot make a very long speech, but I will try my best." Repeatedly his advisers and friends urged him to end his speech, but he waved them off and finished.[2]

Often this is how we believe that our demeanor and actions should be on a detour. We have not been shot, but we feel that if we are stubborn, determined, and resilient enough we can get through anything. Those of us in the church have taken this idea and spiritualized it. Modern-day Christians have turned the expression "When the going gets tough, the tough get going" into "When the going gets tough, the tough read their Bibles daily, pray without ceasing, do not worry, rejoice in the Lord, pretend that everything will be okay, put money in the plate, and get going." Now, every one of those things is good and right, but too often we treat things that are good and right as tasks that must be completed in order to finish our detour. We convince ourselves that God has let this happen to me so that I can learn how to *do* something more or better, and when I learn the lesson the detour will end. As a result, our best efforts to end our detour often leave us exhausted, worried, and struggling to emerge from circumstances that only seem to spiral us further downward.

Our Christian culture seems to be fascinated with this tendency to live life at full throttle. If you are not exhausted, you must not be doing something right, particularly if you are facing adversity or if your life has not gone how you envisioned it. In contrast, Dr. Howard Hendricks, a man who taught seminary classes for almost six decades and kept a schedule in his eighties that would make some thirty-year-olds exhausted, writes, "Someone says, 'Don't you know it's better to burn out than to rust out?' This is spiritual nonsense, for that's not the option. It's not a question of burning out or rusting out, it's a question of living out. And that takes the balance of the ministry of the Holy Spirit."³ In other words, burning out and rusting out are not the only options: Christians need to find the balance between laziness and never slowing down.

At any time, but particularly when you are on a detour, it can seem spiritual to essentially abuse yourself trying to rectify the situation. You either forgo meals or your diet is horribly unhealthy, you lose sleep, and you spend all of your time trying to think and work yourself out of the situation. It feels spiritual, and you tell yourself that it is, but all you are really doing is abusing your own body and continuing a downward spiral.

Paul tells us that "the body is the temple of the Holy Spirit" (1 Corinthians 6:19). Those who pressure you to go without sleep, exhaust yourself participating in every ministry possible, and attend every church event even if you do not have the time are not considering your physical well-being. Warren Wiersbe reminds us,

> Take care of your body. Late hours, overweight, fast food lunches, constant pressure—all these can create physical problems that affect your mind and emotions. Sometimes the most spiritual thing you can do is take a nap! (Consider Elijah in 1 Kings 19.) Your body is God's temple and God's tool—take care of it. You need a day off and a vacation, just like any other workman.⁴

Now there are people in our lives who have some or most of the problems they do because they are lazy or careless. I am not advocating an approach to detours that neglects accountability or responsibility, nor am I suggesting that detours are to be laid-back vacations. However, many of us are like Elijah. We are doers who approach detours as problems to be defeated. For those of us like Elijah, a detour may be God's way of forcing us to do what we needed to do all along, like take better care of ourselves mentally, spiritually, and physically.

Certainly there must be a balance. Some people foolishly believe that life is just one big vacation. That attitude of entitlement flies in the face of a biblical work ethic that tells us that hard work is vital and important. The book of 2 Thessalonians goes so far as to say, "If anyone is not willing to work, then he is not to eat, either" (3:10). Yet the same Bible tells us in Genesis 2:3 that, from the beginning of creation, God intended for man to have periods of rest and recuperation. To neglect rest is just as serious and against God's plan as to neglect work.

Note in 1 Kings 19:5–7 that God did not tell Elijah to read the Scriptures more, to pray harder, to put together a better marketing plan for his ministry, or to take a couple of classes from the Secret Service on handling death threats. No, instead God in His infinite wisdom saw to it that Elijah's physical needs were met first. Very soon God would deal with the issues in Elijah's heart that had caused him to flee Israel and its vile leaders, but first He saw to it that Elijah had food, water, and rest. It reminds me of a good principle I once heard for sermon length: "The mind can only comprehend what the seat can endure."

On a detour it is counterintuitive to place a high priority on taking care of yourself physically. Everything inside of you is screaming to get to work, to keep looking and searching until you find a way out of your detour. But that is not the example that God himself set when He intervened in Elijah's detour.

STOPPING THE SPIRAL

The parallel between taking one of life's unexpected detours and encountering quicksand is an interesting one, not just because of what not to do, but also because of what you should do. Take a look at this list of what to do if you ever find yourself sinking in quicksand:[5]

1. Avoid quicksand. (If you are already stuck in quicksand, this does not do you much good.)
2. Carry a big stick to test the ground in front of you. (Again helpful before you step in the quicksand, but not as much afterward, although the stick can assist in extricating yourself from the mire. So always make sure you car has a stick in it in case you hit quicksand on your commute.)
3. If you step in quicksand, drop everything. (Get rid of the extra weight—your body is less dense than quicksand so you can only sink so deep without struggling.)
4. Relax. (Easy for the person not in quicksand to say if you ask me.)
5. Breathe deeply. (Again, if I am in quicksand, this might be a tad difficult.)
6. Get on your back. (This makes it harder to sink and will help you to free your legs.)
7. Take your time. (Sure, you are just sinking in quicksand, but this is nothing to get in a hurry about.)
8. Get plenty of rest. (I don't know about you, but were I to be stuck in quicksand, I would find it quite difficult to catch some sleep.)

Now these instructions for getting out of quicksand may seem difficult to follow if you were actually stuck, but they are similar to what we must do in a detour. The urge to fight and struggle is so pronounced that you must be intentional about doing just the opposite.

For most of my life I have had respiratory troubles of one type or another. I have asthma and allergies, and get frequent sinus infections. As a result, when my wife and I go scuba diving, we have two distinct styles underwater. She is graceful, like some strange half human–half fish creature, and she can spend tons of time underwater using little of the oxygen in her tank. She is quite at home in the depths of the sea. I, however, tend to resemble a freight train that has jumped its tracks and landed in the water. I have a bad habit underwater of breathing rapidly and deeply. When we go scuba diving I have to constantly remind myself to breathe slowly and to stay relaxed. If I forget, before you know it my tank of air is running low and I have to surface. While everyone else is exploring beautiful reefs, amazing plant and animal life, and shipwrecks, my dive is already over. The only way that I can swim anywhere near as long as my wife is if I am mindful to control my breathing while I am on the dive. If I do what comes naturally, my dive will be short-lived.

Taking care of yourself during a detour will not come naturally. What is natural is to live on the edge of panic, spending all of your time, energy, and thoughts trying to leave your detour. It will only be through constant, intentional, and focused effort that you will stop your downward spiral.

Being intentional about food and sleep, as well as spiritual disciplines such as Bible study and prayer, is important because it will help you reach a point of stabilization. And it is at this point for Elijah that his detour took a turn. Before Elijah's spiritual and emotional issues can be resolved, his physical needs had to take precedence. He cannot begin moving forward in his detour until he stabilizes. It is only after he is fed and rested that the angel reveals to Elijah that he has an upcoming trip. Nothing in the passage indicates that Elijah had any idea that he would be going anywhere else. Remember, if he had his way God would have killed him under that tree.

Now your detour may follow a similar pattern to Elijah's and it may not. That is why taking care of yourself is so vital to the experience of a detour. You do not know how long you are going to be on this journey. It could last a while. If you do not take care of yourself, you will be ill-prepared and unequipped for the journey ahead of you.

There is a point in a detour that your focus can and should shift from preservation to stabilization and finally to realization. One of the greatest benefits to being intentional about taking care of yourself while in the midst of a detour is that you might learn something. If we, at this point in our detour, are intentional about slowing down and taking care of ourselves, there is a good chance that we will see God at work in places we have never seen Him before. But the opportunity for realization is up to us.

Here we learn from the prophet's poor example. He seems completely unmoved and unfazed by the fact that he has been visited by a mighty angel. You have to wonder if he has missed his lesson, and assume at the least that it is taking him longer to learn it.

Elijah has seen many wonderful and amazing things during his life as a prophet. He has seen droughts caused by God, ravens bringing him bread and meat, a young boy resurrected from the dead because of his prayers, and fire coming down from heaven. Yet the visit from this angel does not seem to faze him. We would hope that this angelic visitor would have shocked Elijah back to reality, that he would stand up and say, "Wait a minute. What am I doing here? I serve an awesome and powerful God!" But all we hear from the prophet is ambivalent silence.

Yet, even though Elijah shows no signs of coming around, it is only now, after he has slowed down and gotten some rest and food, that God deals with the true issues that have been plaguing Elijah on his detour thus far. Now that he is fed and rested Elijah is in a place to see what God has for him on the rest of his detour.

QUESTIONS FOR DISCUSSION

1. How often do you feel pressure, from others or yourself, to push yourself beyond your limits?
2. Why is it so hard for us to take care of ourselves, particularly on a detour?
3. What does our propensity to neglect ourselves in detours tell us about ourselves?
4. Why do you think it was so important for God to take care of Elijah physically first?

SIX

DETOURS AND GETTING BACK TO BASICS

1 Kings 19:8-9a

The year that my family and I went to Albuquerque, New Mexico, for vacation was an adventurous one. First, there was the night that we endured borderline tornado-force winds in the little pop-up camper. Next, there was the attempted trip to the Albuquerque zoo. The trip to the zoo, otherwise known as the "map incident" in family lore, was one detour that we did not expect.

On that morning, we loaded in the car and headed off to the famous Albuquerque zoo to see the buffaloes (my dad's favorite), the giraffes (my mom's favorite), and to avoid seeing snakes at all cost (pretty much a unanimous family decision, but a demand that I personally held near and dear). We left the campground with my father driving, my mom in the passenger seat navigating with a map of the city of Albuquerque, and me in the backseat entertaining myself and asking how much longer until I could see the lions and tigers and bears.

We thought it would take only a few minutes to arrive at our destination, but some time passed and we had not found the zoo. We turned around and went back in the other direction, assuming that we had somehow missed it, but we still could not find it. We took a left turn. We took a right turn. We made an illegal U-turn. We made a legal U-turn. We went farther south, farther north, farther east, and farther west, but we were about as close to finding the Albuquerque zoo as we were to landing on the moon.

Slowly the tension and irritation level in the car began to rise, and an impatient child in the backseat surely did not help matters. My mother was doing her best to navigate, but my dad was becoming frustrated as he took turn after turn all over New Mexico. Our scenic tour of the historic Albuquerque dragged on and on, until finally my father had had enough.

Keeping his right hand on the wheel, my dad cranked his window all the way down, and with the fresh mountain air blowing in his hair, he then reached across his body for the map. As he took hold of the map, he said rather shortly to my mother, "Give me that!" and he suddenly threw it out the window. He turned the car around and headed back to the campground.

My dad's impatience and frustration with our detour, two traits he surely did not pass on to his son, had boiled over. Our trip to the zoo had ended without us ever seeing the zoo, and now our map was blowing down historic U.S. Route 66. My dad sped back to our campground while my mom and I tried not to laugh out loud and hoped that we could actually find our campsite. Eventually we arrived safe and sound back at our pop-up camper. We had managed to retrace our steps to the beginning, but our detour had been so frustrating that we just gave up on trying again.

Often if a detour continues for some time you can become impatient, frustrated, and discouraged. It may seem like your detours have detours of their own. You begin to wonder if you will ever find your way back to your original destination, and sometimes you cannot even remember where you were headed in the first place. The mistake that we made looking for the zoo (okay, there were really several mistakes, but we will just focus on one) was that we never went back to our point of origin and retraced our steps. We probably just took one wrong turn, and were not able to find our way because of it. Retracing your steps enables you to start at the beginning, figure out exactly where you are coming from, and maybe regain some idea of where you are going.

First Kings 19:8–9 finds Elijah taking a journey, and even though he might not have known it at the start of the journey, God is taking him back to his roots, back to where it all began.

So he arose and ate and drank, and went in the strength of that food forty days and forty nights to Horeb, the mountain of God. Then he came there to a cave and lodged there. (1 Kings 19:8–9a)

Elijah emerged from his sleep and began a journey farther south. He had fled from the land of Israel and passed through the southernmost part of the land of Judah. Now, still all alone, he proceeds to a mountain referred to as Horeb. This trip has a remarkable amount of depth for us to consider.

First, the amount of time it takes Elijah to journey further southward is significant. The distance from Beersheba to Mount Horeb was approximately two hundred miles. Elijah was already a little bit south of Beersheba when he began his journey, so that distance would have been slightly smaller. Still, for one man to walk that distance in that part of the world would have taken at least two weeks. It took Elijah forty days, which is a clear parallel to Moses and the children of Israel. As one commentary describes it, "Moses and the Israelites had traveled in that wilderness for 40 years, sustained by the manna God had provided for them and learned lessons of His faithful care and provision. Now Elijah would traverse the same desert for 40 days and . . . nights, sustained by the bread God provided and would learn the same lessons."[1] Even though Elijah had heard stories of God sustaining His people, and had staked his life on his belief in God's power based on the stories of Israel's exodus from Egypt, he now needed to learn reliance on God's provision firsthand.

Second, Elijah's planned destination is significant. Horeb is a geographical name with which the average Bible reader is probably not familiar. We have all heard of Jerusalem, Bethlehem, and the Jordan River, but Horeb is not nearly as well-known, or at least not by that name. In the Old Testament it was at Horeb that God called to Moses in the burning bush (Exodus 3:1–12), and it is typically referred to by another name—Mount Sinai. Again there is an intentional effort by the writer of 1 Kings to show a similarity between Elijah and Moses. Moses had been called by God and had led the people of Israel. It was under his leadership that the people had received the law from God, even though the people proved to be largely unfaithful. Elijah had been called by God and had attempted to lead the people of Israel. Elijah had sought to turn the people back to the law of God, but the people and their leadership had proved to be largely unfaithful.

The writer of 1 Kings portrays Elijah as "a second Moses," and his trip to Sinai is important for this reason.

Elijah is in crisis and wants to terminate both his prophetic ministry and his life. In an act of sheer grace God intervenes, provides the prophet with life-giving food and water, and suggests a pilgrimage to Mount Sinai, the place that is forever associated with the source and essence of Israelite faith.[2]

For the Israelites, Mount Sinai is associated with "covenant-making, God's revelation of the Torah, and construction of the tabernacle."[3] The importance of this mountain cannot be overstated.

Many religions of Elijah's day found significance in mountains. These ancient people groups associated worshipping their particular deity with mountaintops.

In Canaanite mythology, Baal was depicted as living on a mountain in the north . . . It is striking that after the confrontation with the prophets of Baal, God took Elijah south, the opposite direction of Baal's dwelling, to the place where the nation of Israel was born when God entered into covenant with those who had left Egypt. It was in effect a geographic way of distancing Israel's faith from all that Baalism represented.[4]

Elijah could not miss the symbolism in where God had taken him. He went to the location that represented the beginning of the nation of Israel's relationship with God, a place that would make possible his later personal relationship with God.

Third, the cave is significant. We have already seen that Elijah in many ways represented a second coming, so to speak, of Moses. What we often miss in the Elijah story is another link between the prophet and Moses—the cave. In Exodus 33:22, while on the same mountain, God places Moses in the "cleft of the rock" when He passes by Moses, and it is entirely possible that Elijah has been taken to the very same place. One scholar writes, "The English text of 1 Kings 19:9 is not as direct as it might be. 'Then he came there to *a* cave' would be rendered more literally as 'Then he came there to *the* cave.' The Hebrew is definite, and a study of the word 'cave' in Hebrew literature suggests that this word with the article is regularly specific rather than generic."[5] When you consider that Elijah was not just headed to "a cave" on Mount Sinai, but "the cave," we can conclude that God likely took Moses to the exact same place where Moses himself experienced God in a unique way.

So the discouraged and downtrodden prophet has traveled for an amount of time that is reminiscent of Moses' time in the wilderness, he has come to the same general location where Moses traveled, and he has come to the exact location in which Moses saw God. In many respects it was there, on that mountain and in that cave, that the Hebrews learned about God. God's revelation of himself and the Old Testament laws and regulations for which Elijah fought so stringently against the prophets of Baal had their earthly origin exactly where the prophet's dusty sandals now resided. Elijah's personal faith, his prophetic vocation, and his identity could trace their lineage here. This is where the nation of Israel began to take its first baby steps as a people following God. It is also where they experienced their first big stumble. Elijah has come back to the beginning, and here at the beginning Elijah will start over. Like many of our detours Elijah has gone a long way, just to get to the starting line.

When God sent Elijah to Mount Sinai, it was very intentional. In a subtle way, before God has even spoken, He has already begun to reach out to Elijah. Was Elijah's frustration with God, and with what God had allowed to happen, in line with who God was and who He had revealed himself to be? That question was at the heart of Elijah's forty-day journey to possibly the very cave to which the Israelite faith could trace itself.

For those of us on a detour, Elijah's example of tracing his steps is important. Though it is not explicitly stated in the passage, I would like to suggest that the prophet's trip to Mount Horeb was done at God's direction. Elijah had already gone as far as he intended to go. He had gone a day's journey past Beersheba into the desert. There, under a tree, he asked to die. Elijah had no intention in going any farther. Also, in verse 7 the angel of God mentions to Elijah that he has an upcoming journey. For these two reasons, the rest of this chapter operates under the assumption that Elijah proceeded to Horeb at God's direction rather than of his own initiative.

WHY RETRACE YOUR STEPS?

So what difference does it make to the person on a detour whether Elijah's trip to Horeb was at God's calling? It makes a difference because, for the person on a detour, retracing your steps may be the first time that you begin to see God's involvement in your detour.

People wind up on a detour for one of two reasons. The first reason is because of our own mistakes. Sometimes life has gone differently than we hoped because our own sins and foolish choices have sent it careening out of control. If your detour has been caused by your own sin, then retracing your steps begins with confessing your sins to God and those you have hurt, and making restitution with those people against whom you have sinned. Until you have done that, you will be stuck on your detour, or life will just be one big detour after another until God has gotten your attention and you become serious about dealing with your sins and shortcomings. The second reason that we may be on a detour is due to a much more ambiguous reason—life happens. Sometimes life gets crazy and things go drastically wrong because that is what life is like in a fallen world, even for believers in Jesus Christ. As was mentioned in chapter 2, we understand why people who do bad things end up on detours, but we can have a difficult time grasping why those of us who are not suffering for sins are on a detour.

That is why retracing our steps on a detour is so important mentally, emotionally, and spiritually. Retracing our steps shifts the focus of the detour to God. Ultimately, if we are on a detour, we are there because of God. While theologians have argued for thousands of years about the relationship of God's sovereignty and human will, it seems fairly safe to say that the person is on a detour either because God has caused it to happen, or because God has allowed it to happen.

Think of retracing your steps like this. Let's say you and a friend are hiking in the woods. You have been on the hike for a few hours when the two of you decide that it is time to turn around and return home. It is then that you realize that you have no idea where you are, or how in the world you are going to get back home. You have no compass, no GPS system, no map, and you are not good with directions. The sun is setting quickly, and it is beginning to get cold. You begin to panic, your mind quickly considers all of the worst-case scenarios, and you deeply regret never becoming a Boy or Girl Scout. Just as you are pondering what your friends and family will say at your funeral, your friend speaks up and tells you not to worry, he has been marking the trail the whole time. Your progress and the path that it took have been tracked the entire time.

A detour is not what you wanted, and it is most certainly not what you planned for, but all along the way God has planned, prepared, and provided for your steps. Retracing your steps starts the process of discovering how God has marked your path.

HOW TO RETRACE YOUR STEPS

I used to have a rather large, moody, and quite possibly mentally disturbed Siamese cat named Simon. Periodically the family would be sitting in the living room when the cat would suddenly dart off the couch and run to one side of the house. Then he would run back through the living room and speed to the opposite side of the house. Then he would return to the other side of the house as quickly as possible. This pattern would go on for several minutes until finally Simon would return to his perch on the couch and resume his normal, everyday, lazy behavior. We never knew why the cat did this. My grandmother claimed that it meant he was constipated, but to be honest, she had many theories that were based in something other than reality, so we discounted this idea. We always found it funny and would joke that maybe the cat just remembered that he had a pressing appointment on the other side of the house, but when he got there he remembered that his appointment was on the other side of the house. Being on a detour can be a lot like that. You may find yourself rushing from place to place, wondering why you are there and how you got there to begin with.

Retracing your steps is a response to a detour that is the opposite of Simon the cat. Retracing your steps is taking the time to look at your life in general, and your detour in particular, and to put them in the framework of the Christian faith. Three starting points are to retrace your steps biblically, theologically, and historically.

Retrace Your Steps Biblically

A detour affects you. There is no way around that fact. You might pretend that it doesn't, but the longer that you are on a detour, and the deeper your troubles go, the more you will struggle. One of the biggest struggles that may arise for the person on a detour is reading the Word of God. Reading and studying the Bible becomes more difficult because discouragement, frustration, and despondency all threaten to make the Bible seem less refreshing and more depressing. You read how David could slay a giant, but there seems to be no end in sight to your problems. You cannot find five smooth stones, you can't seem to remember where you placed your slingshot, and you do not even know how to use one anyway. You see Daniel survive the lions' den, and you wonder how that is supposed to apply to your life. Daniel did not seem worried about the lions, but you feel like your problems will never end, and even if they do, you do not know whether you can recover from them. When you compare yourself to the people of the Bible, you just do not seem to measure up.

Because of this, when you do read the Bible, you tend to read it like a shipwreck survivor looking for land. Instead of reading the text carefully, taking the time to study it and glean the meaning, you hurriedly skim passages looking for some kind of a command from God to tell you what to do, or for some spiritual secret that will make everything make sense. Instead of looking for God, you are looking for secret codes and messages that will help you make sense of your specific problems and find a way past them.

For the person experiencing a detour, retracing your steps includes looking for patterns in the Bible rather than personal messages. Remember our friend Elijah—a major part of God helping the prophet retrace his steps was to take him on a similar journey to that of Moses. Instead of reading the Bible looking for answers, read the Bible looking for similarities to your own life and situation. All of God's children go on detours, and those who followed God in the Bible had some real doozies. Even though the world and everyday experiences of those in the Bible were far different from our own, seeing a pattern to how God dealt with them can be a tremendous help in seeing how God similarly deals with us. Consider these examples of patterns that might be similar to your detour:

- Do things seem to go from bad, to worse, to worst? Try looking into Joseph (Genesis 37, 39–40).
- Did your entire life turn upside down in one tragic moment? Meet my friend Job (Job 1–2).
- Have some of your own sinful decisions wrecked your life? King David is your man (2 Samuel 11–12; Psalm 51).
- Did you have a plan for how to do God's will that has not worked out? Moses knows all about it (Exodus 2).
- Are you in a position that is perilous and hazardous? Queen Esther is a good place to start (Esther 4).

The list of people who loved God and followed Him through a detour could go on and on. Reading your Bible looking for these patterns will help you begin to see that not only are you not alone on your detour, but in many cases the road you are walking is actually a well-beaten path.

Retrace Your Steps Theologically

At first glance it may seem confusing to separate retracing your steps biblically from retracing your steps theologically. After all, all good theology emanates from the Bible, so what is the difference? Well, for our purposes we are going to think of theology as an overarching idea in the Bible as opposed to one particular story or character. So first, retrace your steps by seeing how the life of Jeremiah, for example, was similar to yours, and then retrace your steps by looking for the Bible's big ideas that relate to your detour.

Often these big ideas help us because on a detour we have a tendency to understand the Bible to say exactly what we want it to say. We want God to heal us so we read verses that promise healing and ignore those that say how God can allow us to suffer for His glory. We want to get out of a painful situation so we read passages where God told someone to leave, and we skip over passages that tell us the value of perseverance.

Along with looking for patterns while reading the Bible, spend time looking for ideas and concepts. If your detour involves facing intense opposition, even though you are in the right, concluding that God wants you to take a slingshot to those people just because you read the story of David and Goliath is bad theology. David, in a specific context, was perfectly in God's will attacking an enemy soldier with a slingshot, but Jesus, Paul, Daniel, Isaiah, and Jeremiah all faced opposition as well. What does the entire Bible say and teach about handling opposition?

When we retrace our steps theologically, we begin to see a bigger picture. Suddenly God's glory and purposes come into view more clearly and our tendency to see what we want to see in the Bible is diminished.

Retrace Your Steps Historically

The person on a detour often has a lot of regrets. No matter the cause of the detour, you can spend all kinds of time and energy thinking about what you could have done differently so that you would not have ended up on your unexpected journey. Add to that how every day you come up with dozens of options for how to get out of the detour, and before long life can become a repeating cycle of analysis, regret, and what-ifs.

That is why it is helpful to retrace your steps historically. Now by historically I am not referring to where your life fits with Winston Churchill, Jackie Robinson, or Ronald Reagan. I am instead referring to your own personal history. Retracing your steps historically asks the question, "Where does my detour fit in my life?" Retracing your steps may not tell you exactly what you want to know, which is, "Why is God allowing this to happen to me?" But it will help you see two things that are very important: repetition and significance.

Odds are that your current detour is eerily reminiscent of a few of your previous detours. This is important because it will tell you something about how God teaches and deals with you. When you retrace your steps biblically and theologically, you will see that God's way of dealing with people is often as diverse as those people themselves. If you are able to see some repetition in your experience, it will help you to understand the pattern and a piece of God's plan.

If you look back over your life and come to the conclusion that your current detour fits a pattern, then you must ask yourself if God has been teaching you a lesson that you have failed to learn. Or, if your detour does not fit any pattern, is it possible that God has a different lesson for you to learn that your current detour has put you in the best position to learn? Many of us have a bad habit of only learning from God and genuinely turning to Him when we are forced to do so. Is this detour a way for God to place you in a situation where you have no choice but to turn to Him?

Placing the detour you are on in the context of your life helps you to see repetition and patterns, but it can also help you to see the possible significance of your detour. There is an old saying that "A bend in the road is not the end of the road, unless you fail to make the turn." Like it or not, your detour has changed your life, not just immediately, but more than likely from this point on. Instead of focusing on why God allowed this to happen to you, ask yourself, "What could God be trying to accomplish in me through this detour?"

A detour is your life making an unexpected, and almost always unwanted turn. Retracing your steps begins the process of realizing that with God, even the most negative of circumstances can have significance, both in the present day and eternally. This is important for us to remember because, as we are about to see, detours can play tricks on us, and sometimes it is hard to determine exactly what is true.

When you are on a detour, just as our friend Elijah was, retracing your steps is often one of the most important things that you can do. Though there will be times on detours when God appears to be silent, we must remember the words of Psalm

46:1, "God is a safe place to hide, ready to help when we need him" (*The Message*). When we feel separated from God, we must remember that God has not gone anywhere and He desires to help us in times of trouble. For the first part of Elijah's detour God was remarkably absent; even when He intervened He only did so by sending an angel to give Elijah food and water. Now God has directed Elijah to a new destination. His request to die under a tree has been denied, and God will soon meet with him face-to-face.

QUESTIONS FOR REFLECTION

1. What patterns do you see in your walk with God?
2. Why can it be difficult for those on a detour to read the Bible carefully, paying attention to context?
3. What do our frequent failures to deal with stress properly tell us about ourselves?
4. What does it tell us about God that in a detour, He brings Elijah, and often us, back to the beginning?

SEVEN

DETOURS AND REALITY

1 Kings 19:9b-10

One of the most overlooked contributions to the effort of Allied Forces in World War II was made by a group of artists, designers, architects, and sound engineers. Officially the motley crew of 1,100 soldiers was named the 23rd Headquarters Special Troops, but unofficially, to the few that knew their methods and activities, they were known by another name—the Ghost Army.

Just after the Allies landed in Normandy, France, the 23rd Headquarters Special Troops was sent near the front lines. Under the cover of darkness, the Ghost Army inflated rubber tanks, jeeps, and airplanes. Through very large speakers they played sound effects that simulated troop and artillery movement and even bridge construction. The soldiers repeatedly changed uniforms and constantly painted different insignia on their inflatable equipment. Periodically the soldiers of the 23rd Headquarters Special Troops, wearing their fake uniforms, were sent into towns and villages across Europe to have a good time and spread the word that whatever division's uniform they happened to be wearing was in the area and on the move.

For twenty missions the Ghost Army did its job to perfection. Then, in late March of 1945, they pulled off their greatest deception of the war. With the Allied forces approaching the border to Germany, the Ghost Army was once again called upon to fool the enemy with a fake army. The 23rd Headquarters Special Troops were tasked with distracting the German army from the location in which the Allies were intending to cross the Rhine River and enter Germany.

Operation Viersen would take all of the ingenuity and creativity that the Ghost Army could muster. They started by traveling in the direction of the south end of the Rhine River in simulated convoys. When they arrived at the river, the 23rd then began to assemble some six hundred inflatable tanks as well as inflatable pieces of artillery. Loudspeakers blasted sounds of trucks and tanks moving, some of which could be heard for over a dozen miles. Then they played sounds of construction and even started building a bridge across the river. Finally they set off flash canisters that would make the Germans think that the 23rd was firing at them. The deception was so thorough that the Germans often returned fire, and periodically damaged one of the "tanks," sending the Ghost Army into a frenzy to patch up the faux armor.

All along, the 23rd was playing fake radio messages from people alleging to be part of the 30th Division and the 79th Division of the United States Army. Their goal was to convince the Germans that those two divisions were going to cross the Rhine dozens of miles south of where they truly intended to cross. As the Germans reinforced their positions and eavesdropped on fake radio transmissions, the Ghost Army moved its fake forces and simulated preparations for a river crossing. At the same time, the real 30th and 79th divisions crept quietly toward the Rhine River far north of where the Germans expected.

When the 30th and 79th divisions finally crossed the Rhine River, the Germans were taken completely by surprise. Not only did they not expect an attack from these divisions, but they did not even know that the 30th and 79th were in the vicinity. German soldiers interrogated after the battle confirmed that virtually all of their commanders had been confident that the attack would come south of where it actually came. The deception was so total that a captured German map showed the 79th division located south; the 30th division was not even on the map.

The deception of the Ghost Army was so effective that it saved thousands of American lives. The estimates of exactly how many lives were saved vary, but Lieutenant General W. H. Simpson, who wrote the Ghost Army a commendation for their efforts, speculated that the lives of as many as ten thousand American servicemen were saved by the well-coordinated deception perpetrated by the 23rd Headquarters Special Troops.

The German army had been caught by surprise because they believed that hundreds of inflatable tanks and jeeps, accompanied by very loud soundtracks, were a real army. The Germans had expected to see tanks and so they saw tanks. They had expected to hear the sounds of construction and so they heard sounds of construction. They had been duped by a group of soldiers who carried few guns, spent most of their time inflating balloons, and had more speakers than bullets.

When we are on a detour, our ability to discern reality can often become compromised. Like those German soldiers shooting at inflatable tanks, our ability to discern exactly what is real can quickly become fuzzy. We can become very sure of what may not be true, and we can just as easily doubt what is most definitely true. Take our friend Elijah, for instance. In the last half of verses 9 and 13 of 1 Kings 19, God asks Elijah a question, not once but twice, and the detoured prophet's answer shows us a lot about detours and our perception of reality.

> *And behold, the word of the Lord came to him, and He said to him, "What are you doing here, Elijah?" He said, "I have been very zealous for the Lord, the God of hosts; for the sons of Israel have forsaken Your covenant, torn down Your altars and killed Your prophets with the sword. And I alone am left; and they seek my life, to take it away." . . . And behold, a voice came to him and said, "What are you doing here, Elijah?" Then he said, "I have been very zealous for the Lord, the God of hosts; for the sons of Israel have forsaken Your covenant, torn down Your altars and killed Your prophets with the sword. And I alone am left; and they seek my life, to take it away."*

Elijah has traveled a long way and is residing in a cave on Mount Sinai. There, he and God begin a question and answer session. When God speaks it reveals a lot about *who* He is, and when Elijah speaks it reveals a lot about *where* he is. We will consider verse 14 along with verses 9 and 10. The reason for this method will be apparent later, but for now let's just focus on the question that God asks and the answer that Elijah gives, identical both times.

God's question, "What are you doing here, Elijah?" is significant for Elijah for two reasons. First, it is significant for what it is not. Second, it is significant for what it is.

To begin, let us look at what God's first words to the prophet Elijah are not. Just as when God initially sent His angel to give the sleeping prophet food and water, God is not vengeful or judgmental. Elijah has abandoned his people, his ministry, and has even asked to die, but God has yet to openly rebuke His faltering prophet. It could be that God's words to Elijah are a more subtle form of rebuke, but it seems that God's question has a different motivation than chastising of the prophet. God is not seeking information that He does not know—after all, God is all-knowing—rather, when God asks questions in the Bible, it is often for the benefit of the person being asked. Consider the words of expert interviewer John Swatsky about questions being like a window that looks out on a lake: "A clean window gives a perfect view. When we ask a question, we want to get a window into the source. People shouldn't notice the question in an interview, just like they shouldn't notice the window. They should be looking at the lake."[1]

God's question to Elijah is not a rebuke but an effort to direct the prophet's thoughts and emotions toward the real issues. God is correcting Elijah, but He is also causing him to reflect on his situation. At this point Elijah is concerned with circumstances and results. His concerns are for the people who refuse to repent, Israel's immoral leadership, and the threat on his life. God has far deeper concerns. Elijah is focused on his own failure, but God's question is intended to bring other issues to the fore.

Elijah's answer is significant because it shows that Elijah's perspective on reality has been affected. Elijah claims that, "I have been very zealous for the Lord, the God of hosts; for the sons of Israel have forsaken Your covenant, torn down Your altars and killed Your prophets with the sword. And I alone am left."

Elijah has been a prominent figure in attempting to turn Israel back to God, but was he the only one in all of Israel zealous for God? In 1 Kings 18:13, when Elijah returned to the land of Israel after having been gone for the three years of drought, he met with Obadiah, a man who followed God and supervised the palace. Obadiah told Elijah that when Ahab and Jezebel were killing the true prophets of God, he "hid a hundred prophets of the Lord by fifties in a cave, and provided them with bread and water."

Elijah was not alone in his zeal for God. There were at least a hundred other prophets alive who were also following God, and Elijah knew that. Even though Elijah knew that he was not alone in his mission to turn the people to God, in the midst of his detour he forgot what he once knew. As Dr. Howard Hendricks writes of this episode in the life of Elijah, "Whenever you have distorted perspective, you always become dishonest, even in your praying."[2] Elijah became so focused on his own needs and difficulties that they have obscured his view of the world and his ability to properly comprehend it. Elijah now has a problem discerning reality. He thinks he is "indispensible to God," but as Dr. Hendricks writes, "he is only an instrument." He continues, "God wants to use you, but the danger is that when He does use you, you begin to think you are the one doing it rather than He. I am convinced that periodically God removes an individual in order to convince us afresh that this is not our work but His."[3] It is certainly plausible that one of God's purposes in allowing Elijah to abandon his post was to teach the prophet that God's work did not revolve around him.

In order for us to relate our detours to that of Elijah, let's consider our culture's perception of reality, how detours can affect our perception of reality, and ways that we can maintain a proper perspective, even during a detour.

OUR CULTURE AND REALITY

In the twenty-first century reality can be something of a fuzzy concept. Discerning reality is more difficult than ever because there are so many new ways to fool people. Consider the following stories taken from the news of the past few years:

- At the 2000 Olympics in Sydney, American athlete Marion Jones won five gold medals. Seven years later she admitted that she had performed so well from the effects of performance-enhancing drugs. As a result, she forfeited all of her medals and prizes. Jones is one of a large number of famous athletes who have cheated via the use of performance-enhancing drugs. Some former baseball players have suggested that the percentage of baseball players using these drugs, until more stringent regulations were instituted, ranged from 25 to 80 percent.[4]

- According to a 2004 story in the *Washington Post*, reality television is not actually real (shocker!). The article states, "The shows are written. They have scripts, called 'paper cuts' in the trade. Jokes are penned for hosts, banter for judges. Plot points and narrative arcs are developed. In some cases, lines are fed directly to contestants . . . reality stories have a beginning and middle and end, shaped by writers who are called not writers but 'story editors' or 'segment producers,' who use the expression 'frankenbites' (after Dr. Frankenstein's monster) to describe the art of switching around contestant sound bites recorded at different times and patched together to create what appears to be a seamless narrative."[5]

- After the advent of the TV show *CSI* (*Crime Scene Investigation*) in the year 2000, colleges across the country saw a jump in the number of students in their forensics departments. Many of these students selected this major based upon what they saw on the show, which is not an accurate portrayal of the profession. Said one university's professor of anthropology, "*CSI* has a lot of technology that doesn't exist. They pull a screen out of thin air and can pull it with their finger, and there are hologram images. Not even close to something that exists. Even if it did exist, there is not a forensic scientist in the world that could afford it. Forensic scientists usually work with a small budget. It's a little bit comical."[6]

- In September of 2009 controversy erupted over the image of musician Kelly Clarkson on the cover of *SELF* magazine. According to the *San Francisco Chronicle*, "Kelly Clarkson was stunned by her own appearance on the recent cover of a fitness magazine because the photograph was so heavily airbrushed, she barely recognized herself. Clarkson has battled weight issues ever since she won the talent show 'American Idol' in 2002, and sparked a furor after appearing on the front of *Self* magazine's September issue looking suspiciously svelte. The editor of the publication defended the decision to airbrush Clarkson, insisting they just wanted to show the singer looking her 'best.' Now Clarkson has opened up about the controversy, admitting she was shocked by the pictures, but accepts all photo shoots inevitably involve the airbrush."[7] Clarkson is one of many popular stars who have been involved in a controversy involving airbrushing. Airbrushing might remove scars, bruises, or tattoos. It might shrink hips, thighs, and stomachs. It might even be used to lighten or darken skin tone.

In America, we are constantly barraged by images and sounds that tell us that they represent reality. We are told that we must look and act like celebrities who spend thousands of dollars on plastic surgery every year to change their appearance and whose appearance on magazines is changed. Children grow up immortalizing and imitating athletes because of their awesome athletic feats, which are fueled by performance-enhancing drugs. And we are entertained by reality television shows that are often scripted and edited to tell a story different than what really happened.

DETOURS AND PERSPECTIVE OF REALITY

With all that society presents as "real," it is pretty obvious that we often encounter something that is less than authentic in our daily lives. On a good day a person must be discerning and led by the Spirit to see through the false realities that are presented, but a detour makes discernment even tougher because your vision can be clouded by the emotion and frustration you feel at being on a detour. I played basketball in a small school in junior high, and our team lost a lot. Every basketball season ended with a tournament, and since we were one of the worst teams, we would play one of the best teams at the beginning. Typically our stay in the tournament was very short. One year, just before the tournament, I made the switch from glasses to contacts. I was thankful for a lot of reasons, not the least of which was that it was so much easier to play basketball in contacts.

The day of the tournament came and I prepared as usual. Even though our team was not expected to win, we did have a chance. I was good at shooting the ball from long distances. If I got on a roll, we could defeat the best team in our district. As the game began, however, I could tell that something was not quite right. My shots were off by just a hair, and I was missing baskets that I would usually make. My clue that something was really wrong was that the scoreboard looked fuzzy, but I assumed that was because I was working hard and sweating a lot. I missed shot after shot that day, until finally the game mercifully ended. We had been demolished by the other team, and I had had an awful day.

A couple of days after the tournament I made a significant discovery when I went to my regularly scheduled optometrist appointment. There was a good reason why I shot the ball so poorly, and why the scoreboard was a little fuzzy during that basketball game—I had accidentally switched my contacts the morning before the tournament. Even though everything looked mostly right, switching my contacts had shifted my perspective just enough that it made me a very poor basketball player. (Thankfully I was not old enough to drive!) In many ways that is exactly what happens to our perspective when we are on a detour. Everything looks and feels like we have a good perspective, but that may not be the case.

When our journey takes a detour, we may simply assume that how we feel and think on the detour is how things actually are.

If God seems far away, then we can quickly forget those times that God has seemed so close and assume that God always has been, and always will be, far away. If our detour has us waiting on financial provision from God, we can easily forget all of those times when He has provided for us and instead focus only on the here and now.

It is this skewed perspective that threatens to lengthen Elijah's detour, taking him even farther off course. When our perspective has been thrown off by a detour, even the slightest change can have negative long-term effects. Like a navigator whose slightly inaccurate calculations take him far from his intended destination, so our skewed perspectives lead us away from where we want to be. When life has taken what we view as a wrong turn, often we try to correct our course to get back on the path on which we want to be. We desperately try to make changes to end the detour and return life to a place of normalcy. However, if our perspective is off, these decisions and choices that we make to end our detour may instead prolong it.

In the late 1960s, psychiatrists Thomas Holmes and Richard Rahe developed what has become known as the Holmes and Rahe Stress Scale. This stress scale was created to determine a person's stress level and to have some sort of an indicator as to whether stressful circumstances might result in illness. They found that the top ten stressors are death of a spouse, divorce, marital separation, imprisonment, death of a close family member, personal injury or illness, marriage, dismissal from work, marital reconciliation, and retirement. Interestingly, when someone endures one of life's most stressful events, they seek to cope by making changes. Unfortunately those changes tend to add more stress to their situation. Be careful about making big changes while you are on a detour. For someone with a fuzzy perspective on reality, it may not be the best idea.

Even though Elijah knew that there were other prophets of God who had not worshipped Baal, in the midst of his detour that detail was seemingly forgotten because his perspective on God, his life, and his situation had become skewed. Elijah experienced what many on a detour experience—the tension and inner battle between what they know to be true and how they feel. Elijah knew he was not the only prophet, but he felt like the only one. In your detour you may know that you have good friends, that God loves you, and that life will not always be like it is for you at that moment, but you do not feel that way. It is these feelings that can really throw off your perspective of reality.

MAINTAINING PERSPECTIVE, EVEN ON A DETOUR

To the person on a detour, a skewed perspective comes from being in a situation that consumes you and does not allow you to see outside of that situation. If you are unemployed, it can become hard to visualize ever finding a job. If you are battling health issues, it becomes difficult to imagine being healthy and vibrant again. If your marriage is in tatters, it is all but impossible to think that your relationship with your spouse could ever be whole again. On a detour you must struggle to maintain a balanced perspective. Let's look at three things you can do to maintain a clear view of reality, even in the most tumultuous of detours.

Retrace Your Steps Again, and Again, and Again

Yes, retracing your steps was discussed in the previous chapter, but it is important to see the link between retracing your steps and maintaining a proper perspective on reality. Retracing our steps reminds us of where we have come from, and remembering that helps to maintain a healthy perspective, even in a detour. Picture someone repelling down the side of a mountain. (I am not sure why this is fun to some people, but I will take their word for it rather than trying it myself.) To the person repelling down the mountain, there is no more important bond than that of him or her to the rope. The climber does not use just any old rope, but specially made climbing ropes composed of several strands of heavy-duty, strenuously tested nylon rope.

Every time you sit down and search the Scriptures and your own life to retrace your steps, it is like adding another strand of rope to connect you to a secure foundation. When you force yourself to search God's Word, even when He seems far away and removed from your life, you are strengthening your bond to Him, even if you do not realize it.

Seek Out Good Advisors

It is a frequent scene in books, movies, and television: a ticking time bomb. The bomb never has much time left on the timer, usually just enough time for the hero or heroine to call their associate who knows how to diffuse bombs. The person on the other end of the panicked phone call attempts to calm the scared friend who is sitting in front of the dangerous explosive. They discuss whether to cut the red wire or the green wire, and eventually diffuse the bomb through the careful direction and advice of the person who is not there but knows how to remedy the situation, and who can talk the scared friend through what is going on and what to do about it.

Detours may not include explosives, but at times they sure feel like every day includes another ticking time bomb. Just as when we talked about isolation, one of the keys to maintaining proper perspective is to maintain good relationships with people that can help you to handle these tricky situations. Your perspective may lead you to conclude that you are a failure, God does not care, and there is no hope, but quality relationships will help you to see that your perspective is leading you to wrong conclusions. Advice and counsel from people with a more accurate perspective may help you see that your situation is quite different than you thought previously.

Avoid Making Major Decisions and Changes

Remember the Holmes and Rahe Stress Scale? All of life's stressful events (or detours) have an impact on us. The more stressful events that we are going through at one time, the higher our risk is for suffering sickness and developing an unbalanced perspective. The scale assigns numbers to different life events and then allows you to tally your score. (The test can be found many places online and is best viewed as a starting point for understanding the stressors in our lives.) If your score is above 300, you are considered at risk for illness. If your score is between 150 and 299, you have a moderate risk of illness. And if your score is below 150, you are expected to have only a slight risk of illness.

Many of these life events are unavoidable. You cannot change that your spouse is sick (44 points) or has passed away (100 points). You cannot always change that you are having trouble with your in-laws (29 points), or that you have been dismissed from your job (47 points). But there are other decisions and changes that can and should wait until life has leveled off a little bit. Often we prolong our detours and miss the very reason that God allowed the detour to come into our lives because we are so busy making changes and adjustments trying to get back to a place that feels more secure and safer than our detour. We must remember that our decisions and attempts to make major changes on a detour can be based on a faulty perspective. Only later when we have regained perspective will we realize that we were in no place to bring those changes into our lives.

Now a detour may be God's way of telling you to change some things. If your detour has been caused by your own sin (imprisonment, by the way, is 63 points on the Holmes and Rahe scale), then you definitely need to make changes. If, however, sin is not the cause of your detour, then you need to be very careful and thoughtful about making changes while on a detour. Eventually you may need to make a change in your diet (15 points), or move to a different house (20 points, although in my experience this should be much higher), but while you are struggling through your detour may not be the best time to make these changes. Often we make cosmetic changes hoping that they will have a greater impact than they realistically can.

As the old saying goes, if you put lipstick on a pig, it is still a pig. Your detour may seem about as attractive to you as Old Mac-Donald's pig, but trying to dress it up by making some minor changes will only add to your stress and inability to maintain a balanced perspective in the midst of your detour. We must acknowledge that detours can and will give us a skewed perspective on reality. This is important to realize because, as we are about to learn, we approach every situation, detour or not, with an imperfect understanding.

QUESTIONS FOR DISCUSSION

1. Do you have people in your life that can help you with perspective?
2. Why is it so easy for you to lose sight of reality in a detour?
3. What does our propensity to lose sight of reality tell us about ourselves?
4. Even though God never changes, we still struggle to maintain a proper perspective of Him. Why?

EIGHT

DETOURS AND IMPERFECT UNDERSTANDING

1 Kings 19:15–18

When two people marry, more than just their lives merge. Marriage means the combining of two backgrounds, two sets of expectations, two sets of interests, and two sets of talents and abilities. Whereas before there were two individuals, now there is one couple with two sets of likes and dislikes, passions, and aversions. As a single person, you might decide that you want pizza for supper for no reason other than it is Thursday and you like pizza. As a married person, you now have to anticipate and take into account another person's desires, thoughts, and feelings.

Over the years of my marriage I have tried to explain many things to my wife in the hope that an increased understanding would lead to a greater interest in those things on her part. Ever the optimist, she too has spent hours trying to explain to her stubborn and hard-headed husband her interests and hobbies. At times our attempts to increase one another's understanding have been rousing successes, and at other times we seem to do little to open the windows into one another's worlds.

My wife is a wonderful seamstress, crocheter, and knitter. Over the years I have seen her sewing machine and knitting needles crank out car seat covers, aprons, blankets, hats, scarves, table runners (I am still a little fuzzy on the purpose of a table runner, but I digress), duvet covers, pillows, tutus, bibs, burp cloths, and all manner of crafty items that I never even knew existed. Knitting is not something, for example, that I am interested in on my own. She will tell me that she is doing a purl stitch, or box stitch, or a linen stitch, and I have no idea what that means. Usually it just reminds me of my inability to learn to tie different knots during my short-lived attempt at being a Boy Scout.

I have seen her produce baby blankets that took dozens and dozens of hours. I have seen the frustration that comes from missing a stitch and having to undo a row to go back and repair the mistake. It is at this point that I would throw the ball of yarn in the fireplace, but she manages to patiently go back and fix what was missed and produce a beautiful blanket. Periodically a big project requires me to help out. Whether it is swinging a hammer to put snaps on a car seat cover, helping feed a massive sheet of fabric through the sewing machine, or unrolling some yarn, I have proven to be helpful at times. Then again there was also the time that I managed to pull down an entire bolt of fabric on my head at a fabric store, so I may not really be all that helpful. Still, the more of these projects that she has done, the more that my exposure to them has given me understanding and in turn appreciation for what it takes to actually knit a blanket.

Conversely, I have attempted to educate my wife in the things of my world, which means learning the sport of football. She knows that I love to watch football, and so she "endures" Sunday afternoons of me tensely yelling at the television because someone dropped a pass or missed a tackle. I regale her with stories of the greatest players ever, telling her how former San Francisco 49er quarterback Joe Montana once started a game-winning drive in the Super Bowl by pointing out famous people in the stands to his nervous teammates. I recite for her how Dallas Cowboys' quarterback Roger Staubach was so artful at avoiding would-be tacklers that he was nicknamed "Roger the Dodger." My wife patiently humors me as I tell these stories. Typically, she smiles at me, makes some sort of a comment, and then goes back to knitting another hat and scarf. I try to convince her that she should be more like her maternal grandmother, who once delayed an operation to watch her Dallas Cowboys take on the Minnesota Vikings, but through it all she maintains that she has little interest in football.

Yet there are times on Sunday afternoons when she seems to be getting into a football game. She will put down the knitting needles and ask me why something happened in the game. I will offer an explanation, and then we will go on with our everyday Sunday business of football and knitting, but I know that she is probably paying more attention to the game than she wants to let on. On top of that, sometimes she will make a comment about a game that lets me know that she has begun to understand the game. And even though my lovely wife will never be the football fan that I am, she is gaining a greater appreciation for the game due to her increased understanding.

Now, I will never be a knitter and my wife will probably never be a big-time football fan, but our experiences trying to help someone with an imperfect understanding sheds light on Elijah's interaction with God. All along Elijah has been operating as if he truly understands God and what He is doing in the world, but now God will show him how little has really understood. The prophet has traveled long and far, he has had a meeting with God himself, and now it is time for him to go back to Israel. Let's see what God tells him to do after Elijah has responded in the same way to the question, "Why are you here?"

The Lord said to him, "Go, return on your way to the wilderness of Damascus, and when you have arrived, you shall anoint Hazael king over Aram; and Jehu the son of Nimshi you shall anoint king over Israel; and Elisha the son of Shaphat of Abel-meholah you shall anoint as prophet in your place. It shall come about, the one who escapes from the sword of Hazael, Jehu shall put to death, and the one who escapes from the sword of Jehu, Elisha shall put to death. Yet I will leave 7,000 in Israel, all the knees that have not bowed to Baal and every mouth that has not kissed him." (1 Kings 19:15–18)

Elijah seems to have learned nothing from his experience. Even after he has seen God (to be discussed in chapter 11), he is still adamant that he is alone in his zeal for God, and that his life is in danger because of it.

In this passage, once again we see the contrast between how God deals with people and how we typically deal with each other. Think about that coworker, or fellow student, or person in your family who just never seems to understand the first time around—that is Elijah in this circumstance. Were we to confront Elijah twice and get the same selfish and pitiful answer both times, many of us would be warming up the fireball from heaven, but that is not how God treated His struggling prophet.

Instead of zapping Elijah, God gives him a list of things to do. Many view verses 15–18 as God giving the prophet a second chance, or recommissioning him, so to speak.

In the recommissioning, God highlights the existence of seven thousand Israelites who have not engaged in rituals honoring Baal. Given that the numbers *seven* and *one thousand* are often symbolic numbers of completeness in the Bible (Gen. 4:15; Exod. 12:15; Josh. 6:4; Acts 6:3; Exod. 20:6; Deut. 1:11; Rev. 20:3), *seven thousand* emphasizes the substantial size of the nucleus of God's faithful community. Elijah need not be so discouraged or take himself so seriously because he is far from being the only person committed to the divine cause. In 1 Kings 19 two things bring Elijah out of his state of discouragement and lethargy. One is a new commission from God, and the other is the assurance that God's cause has a future in the world which does not depend only on Elijah's personal success or lack thereof.[1]

Slowly but surely the dark clouds are parting for Elijah. God's presence has become more specific and pronounced as Elijah has been in the wilderness. Look at the chart below that shows the escalation of God's personal involvement in Elijah's detour:

God is:	Unseen and Seemingly Uninvolved				Interacting and Directing Elijah through the Angel of the Lord		Dialoging with Elijah	Personally Commanding Elijah
Verses in 1 Kings 19	1-2	3a	3b	4	5-7	8-9a	9b-14	15-18

GOD UNDERSTANDS

For a time Elijah's detour consisted of what happened to him—Jezebel's threat on his life in verses 1–2, and his reaction to it in verses 3–4. Now at long last God has shown up and seems to be taking charge. How did He go about this?

> In Elijah's experience, as is so often the case with us, God did not remove the burden, but He gave fresh supplies of grace so that the prophet could bear it. He neither took away Jezebel nor wrought a mighty work of grace in the hearts of Israel, but He renewed the strength of His over-wrought servant. Though Elijah had fled from his post of duty, the Lord did not now desert the prophet in his hour of need.[2]

Note that God never answers the question that I would assume to be on Elijah's lips: "Why?"

It should tell us something that the mighty Elijah, one of the Bible's most righteous and outstanding figures, has to relate to God on God's terms. Twice God had asked Elijah what he was doing there, allowing Elijah to reveal his own pride and skewed perspective. Now, having dealt incredibly gently and graciously with his faltering prophet, God confirms and redirects Elijah in verses 15–18. There are three things in particular that God understands but Elijah does not: God understood where Elijah needed to be, God understood who Elijah needed, and God understood what was coming for Elijah.

God Understood Where Elijah Needed to Be

God's first two words to Elijah in verse 15 are very telling, "Go, return." When God tells us to do something, it is different than when we give out orders. We direct people based on what we believe they can and should do. A boss tells his employees to perform a given task believing that they can fulfill the task, but sometimes a boss overrates his employees' abilities or underestimates the difficulty of the given task. Even the most well-intentioned and informed command may be misdirected or faulty. Human directives are always fallible, because we human beings are fallible.

Unlike our commands, God's commands are never at fault and His timing is perfect. When a person breaks a leg, there will come a time when the doctor tells him or her to begin walking on it again. All patients, however, are different, and so it may be that one patient needs more time than another to heal. The doctor cannot know the perfect time to ask the patient to start using the leg. However, when God tells us to do something, then it is the time to do it. Elijah may not have felt ready to return to Israel, but God in His infinite wisdom knew that it was the right time.

God Understood Who Elijah Needed

Elijah's independence and propensity to isolate himself have been constant themes in his detour. Up until this point in his ministry he has reflected the spirit of the old Westerns starring John Wayne that were required viewing for anyone who was at my grandfather's house while they were on TV. Those Westerns were all similar. There were bad guys (who did not shoot guns accurately), and there was the good guy played by John Wayne. John Wayne always shot accurately, and if need be could just throw down his gun and beat up the bad guys. Sometimes John Wayne had a little bit of help, but you always knew that John Wayne could take on all the bad guys by himself if need be, and sometimes that is exactly what he did.

Before his detour Elijah had operated a lot like John Wayne. The bad guys, prophets of Baal, had been taken down by his ministry. Even John Wayne would have been hesitant to fight if the odds were 450–1, but Elijah had killed every one of them. Of course, we know it was the Spirit of God working in Elijah that had defeated those bad guys, but Elijah had begun to take his success personally. Why else would he have run from Jezebel? It is time for Elijah's ministry to take on an associate. Elijah's one-man prophetic band needs to become a duet, and it is for Elijah's good, as well as Israel's.

God Understood What Was Coming for Elijah

For as much as Elijah knew and could discern, he still did not understand tomorrow. God's plan for Elijah and the nation of Israel was far more intricate and far-reaching than the prophet could have ever understood. Whereas Elijah felt that he was a single, solitary soul standing against a wave of idol worship, God had already put plans in motion to eventually break Israel of their destructive habit of worshipping false gods.

This process would not be enjoyable for Israel, but it would be the only way to convince them to return. Elijah had hoped to start a revival to bring Israel back to what it used to be under King David and King Solomon, but that didn't happen. Now Elijah must get over his "good old days" syndrome. God does not want to return Israel to better days gone by, He wants them to return to *Him*.

Elijah will not press forward into an uncertain future alone. He will have Elisha by his side and seven thousand other faithful followers of God as well.

IMPERFECT UNDERSTANDING AND YOUR DETOUR

For the person on a detour, understanding is desperately desired. The person on a detour is frantic to know why God allowed this to happen, what the outcome will be, how it all will end, and what he or she is supposed to learn from it all. However, in order for us to navigate life's detours, we must acknowledge and come to grips with our inability to understand life as God does. We must come to realize in a detour that we simply do not understand what is going on. We want to, we would like to think that we do, but we truly have no idea.

Sometimes we are given some understanding of the purpose of our detour, or at least what we are to learn from it. During one detour that my wife and I experienced involving relationship tension with people with whom we had been close, my wife (usually the spiritual one in the relationship) asked me, "What are you learning from this?" I thought about it for a moment and answered, "I'm not learning anything. I am using all my effort just to not take a swing at someone." On that particular detour my wife was able to see some purpose to the detour, but it would be some time before I was able to have any understanding of God's purpose in the situation.

Often we can become obsessed with trying to determine the purpose of our detour. In all of our searching for the answer to the question of why, we can easily become convinced that maybe there is no purpose. One of the wisest and most profound statements about detours comes to us from the apostle Paul in 2 Corinthians 12:7–10:

Because of the surpassing greatness of the revelations, for this reason, to keep me from exalting myself, there was given me a thorn in the flesh, a messenger of Satan to torment me—to keep me from exalting myself! Concerning this I implored the Lord three times that it might leave me. And He has said to me, "My grace is sufficient for you, for power is perfected in weakness." Most gladly, therefore, I will rather boast about my weaknesses, so that the power of Christ may dwell in me. Therefore I am well content with weaknesses, with insults, with distresses, with persecutions, with difficulties, for Christ's sake; for when I am weak, then I am strong.

The apostle Paul's detour, or as he puts it his "thorn in the flesh," is enlightening for us. In 2 Corinthians 12 we find this mighty apostle asking God to end his detour. Instead of removing the problem, God gives Paul an answer that reveals a two-part purpose for Paul's detour that is applicable to our detours as well. First, God's grace is bigger than any detour. No detour can take you lower than God's grace can reach. It may be that if not for your detour you would never have known just how unsearchable the riches of God's grace are. Second, it is only in our detours, when we are weak, that God can truly prove himself strong. It is one thing to know that God is there, but it is another thing entirely to rely on Him and His wisdom, particularly when you cannot see His plan.

You may know God's purpose for your detour, you may discover the purpose along the way, or you may never know why God has allowed you to take a particular detour. What you can believe, and what you can rest upon, is that there is a purpose. Even if you have an imperfect understanding of what that purpose may be, your detour will allow an opportunity for God's grace and strength to shine in your life.

If you are struggling with an imperfect understanding, there is no magic potion that will help you to see the world and your circumstances as God does, but you can do three things despite your finite understanding. First, get back in the game. Second, find an Elisha. Third, trust God with your uncertain future.

Get Back in the Game

For many years Graham Thomas Chipperfield was a lion tamer with Ringling Bros. and Barnum & Bailey Circus. One day while performing his act he was mauled by one of his lions, a five hundred–pound lioness named Sheba. That certainly qualifies as a detour, and for many of us it would also qualify as a reason to find a new job, but lion tamers have a different way of looking at the world. It took eighty stitches for Chipperfield's doctors to sew up his back, and they advised him to spend the next two months resting and recuperating. Nine days later, however, Chipperfield was back in the cage with Sheba. He explained his actions saying, "I knew that if I stayed out, I would never get back in."[3]

In Elijah's detour, just as with ours, there is a time to be still and know that God is God (see Psalm 46:10). Every detour entails waiting, being patient, and aligning ourselves with God's purposes and desires for our lives. We must, however, be careful that we do not make inactivity and passivity our destination rather than part of the journey. Detours happen for all of us, and during them we may have to go through periods of rest and recovery, but we cannot allow these times of discouragement and frustration to permanently sideline us from what God has for us. In many ways a detour can and will be a very painful experience. Depending on exactly what your detour is, it may take some time for you to recover physically, mentally, and spiritually. Still, there must come a point at which you determine to work through any pain.

Find an Elisha

The ability to surround yourself with spiritually mature believers in Christ can mean the difference between enduring a detour and being overwhelmed by a detour. For Elijah, the emergence of Elisha in his life cannot be overstated for him personally as well as for the well-being of the nation of Israel. From this point on Elisha would serve as an assistant and protégé of the older and more notorious prophet Elijah. Eventually their friendship would culminate in Elisha replacing Elijah as the dominant prophet and voice of God in Israel.

For those of us on a detour, we have learned about the need to avoid isolation, and to find people who will lend perspective to us when we are on a detour. Now we must go a step further. We must also begin to think about life beyond the detour. Even if your detour has no end in sight, you must live and plan as though life will return to normal. A big part of that plan needs to be accountability and continuing to develop relationships that will be beneficial. Detours can cause you to develop tunnel vision with your friendships, meaning you are susceptible to only seeking out people that can help you get out of the situation that you find yourself in. Instead what you should do is develop good, quality friendships that will be long-lasting.

Trust God for an Uncertain Future

The inventions of Thomas Alva Edison, such as the light bulb, have endured for eighty years since he passed from this earth. In 1911, Edison was asked by a reporter to make predictions for the world in 2011, one hundred years later. It is amazing how many of Edison's predictions were true, but many of them were quite far off. Check out these predictions by Mr. Edison.[4]

- In the year 2011 such railway trains as survive will be driven at incredible speed by electricity.
- The house of the next century will be furnished from basement to attic with steel, at a sixth of the present cost—of steel so light that it will be as easy to move a sideboard as it is today to lift a drawing room chair. The baby of the twenty-first century will be rocked in a steel cradle; his father will sit in a steel chair at a steel dining table, and his mother's boudoir will be sumptuously equipped with steel furnishings.
- Books of the coming century will all be printed leaves of nickel, so light to hold that the reader can enjoy a small library in a single volume. A book two inches thick will contain forty thousand pages, the equivalent of a hundred volumes; six inches in aggregate thickness, it would suffice for all the contents of the *Encyclopedia Britannica*. And each volume would weigh less than a pound.
- The day is near when bars of [gold] will be as common and as cheap as bars of iron or blocks of steel . . . Before long it will be an easy matter to convert a truck load of iron bars into as many bars of virgin gold.
- There is no reason why our great liners should not be of solid gold from stem to stern; why we should not ride in golden taxicabs, or substituted [*sic*] gold for steel in our drawing room suites. Only steel will be the more durable, and thus the cheaper in the long run.

Thomas Edison was one of the most intelligent men of modern times. He had a remarkable grasp of electricity, but expectations for gold-plated taxicabs and ocean liners were obviously misplaced.

If a man as smart as Edison failed to understand the future, then it should be of little wonder that our own understanding of what is to come is faulty.

At some point on a detour your faith in God will be forced to move from a luxury to a definite choice. It will not be easy to believe when your are on a detour, particularly as time drags on and there seems to be no end in sight. You will feel like God cannot or will not take care of you. You will want to give up, but you have to make a conscious decision to trust your future, no matter how scary it is, to God.

Thankfully, just as the prophet Elijah, we serve a trustworthy God that is not bound by time and space. While we have an imperfect understanding, God is all knowing. As He asked Job when Job was on a detour, "Where were you when I laid the foundation of the earth? Tell Me, if you have understanding" (Job 38:4). Our lives and our detours are never surprises to God. He knows all and sees all. He was on our detour before we were.

QUESTIONS FOR DISCUSSION

1. What are specific obstacles that you face in understanding God and His plans?
2. Do you worry about the future?
3. What does it tell us about ourselves that we like to pretend we have a better understanding than we really do?
4. What does it say about the trustworthiness of our God that He never suffers from an imperfect understanding?

NINE

DETOURS AND WHAT TO DO

1 Kings 19:19–21

When I was younger I played basketball, lots and lots of basketball. My friends and I played before school, at recess, after school, on the weekends, after church, and at practices and games for our school's team. I had a basketball goal in my backyard, my dad was a coach so he had a key to the school gym, and even my laundry hamper (which mom rightfully claimed was terribly underutilized) was shaped like a basketball goal. I played basketball with friends at the gym throughout college and into my years at seminary; every chance I had I played basketball for exercise and enjoyment. When it came to getting in shape I hated running or jogging, but if you put a basketball in my hands I could run all day.

Then came that fateful day in the spring of 2003. It was Good Friday, and since I did not have class that day I made my way to the gym to play basketball with friends. We had been playing for a while when I landed a little awkwardly and my right knee gave a little. Because of a previous injury years earlier I knew that knee was not very solid. There was some pain and discomfort, but nothing to keep me from continuing to play my favorite game.

Frankly, I was unstoppable that day. I hit shot after shot. My knee was hurting more and more, and still I kept playing. After a few more awkward landings I was all but limping around the court, but I didn't want to stop. Even on one leg I was beating my friends. Then during one play I got the ball, drove to the basket, jumped up, and laid the ball in the basket. As I came down I had my final awkward landing of the day. This time my knee bent the wrong way (just writing about it still creeps me out).

A friend helped me up off the court; my day of basketball was officially over. Back in the dorm, my friend helped me to my room where I elevated my knee and placed an ice pack on my leg. I tried to stay off my feet as much as possible, and I even bought a nice brace with magnets in it that supposedly helped circulation, but all to no avail. My knee simply was not getting better, and so I finally broke down and went to see an orthopedic surgeon.

An X-ray was taken, an examination was performed, and an MRI was endured. Finally I received the bad news. I had completely torn the anterior cruciate ligament (ACL) in my knee. For those who have never had the pleasure of learning about the knee's structure, the ACL is the most important of the knee's four ligaments. It keeps a leg from bending the wrong direction, and connects the bones of the knee joint. I would require surgery to repair the damage to my knee.

As anyone who has ever had ACL reconstruction can attest, recovery can be difficult. Professional athletes can come back from an ACL reconstruction quickly because they have abundant medical facilities, physicians, and time for physical therapy. The average person does not have such resources. I had to recover as quickly as possible so that I could return to work and school. I worked several times a week with a physical therapist who helped me return to my old form, or at least as close to it as possible.

For me one of the most challenging parts of recovery was learning to walk again. Though I had always been a little clumsy, I was decent on my feet before the surgery. After the surgery, however, I had to spend tremendous amounts of time rebuilding the muscles in my leg and retraining myself to walk, something that I had been doing for around twenty-five years at that point.

At the beginning I was a nervous wreck. The doctor told me that the only thing that I could do to mess up my knee during recovery was to fall on it. So as I learned to walk with two legs and two crutches, I was always afraid of falling. Eventually I graduated to using just one crutch, and finally I was back to walking ever so slowly on my two feet. I spent dozens of hours practicing my balance and taking steps where my weight shifted from heel to toe as I walked.

The task of learning how to walk in my mid-twenties was challenging. Despite the fact that I had been walking and running for my whole life, this basic act was difficult for me to relearn. I wanted to be running and jumping, but instead I was taking baby steps. I wanted to be back on the basketball court, but instead I was straining just to navigate stairs.

A frustrating thing about detours is that you desperately want to know what you should do in the situation, but answers to your questions of what to do are hard to come by. You want to know if you should stay or go, if you should try the new treatment or not, if you should accept the new job or stay in your old position, if you should try to reconcile the relationship one more time or not.

In these times of continually asking yourself and God what to do, Elijah's detour can seem of little help. Unlike for you, God showed up personally and gave Elijah specific orders about how to proceed. You would like a personal memo on heaven's letterhead signed by God, but instead all you seem to have are more questions.

Before we dismiss the end of Elijah's journey through the wilderness, however, it would be beneficial for us to examine it more thoroughly.

> *So he departed from there and found Elisha the son of Shaphat, while he was plowing with twelve pairs of oxen before him, and he with the twelfth. And Elijah passed over to him and threw his mantle on him. He left the oxen and ran after Elijah and said, "Please let me kiss my father and my mother, then I will follow you." And he said to him, "Go back again, for what have I done to you?" So he returned from following him, and took the pair of oxen and sacrificed them and boiled their flesh with the implements of the oxen, and gave it to the people and they ate. Then he arose and followed Elijah and ministered to him. (1 Kings 19:19–21)*

To the person on a detour, these last three verses of the story of Elijah's detour can be incredibly annoying. Most of us on a detour spend large amounts of time pondering what we should do, often with what seems like precious little help or information from God. Yet when we read the story, it seems like Elijah's detour, while dramatic and depressing, is short. God does not make him wait long before He gives Elijah some answers. We have to remember that each person's detour will be different. You may be seeking answers, but unlike with Elijah they may never come. That is why it is so important to remember that there is a purpose to your detour. The purpose of your detour may be different than mine, which may be different than someone else's, which may be different than Elijah's.

THE LAST STEPS

In the previous chapter it was suggested that one purpose of Elijah's detour was for the prophet to realize that the world did not revolve around him. "Part of God's response to the discouragement of Elijah is to provide for ongoing prophetic leadership so that Elijah will realize that not everything depends on him. The important point is that through Elijah's return to ministry and the calling of Elisha, the older prophet continues to play a significant role in carrying forward God's purposes."[1]

There are a couple of interesting things to note at the end of Elijah's time in the wilderness. First, God specifically told Elijah to do three tasks in verses 15–16:

- Anoint Hazael king over Aram
- Anoint Jehu the son of Nimshi king over Israel
- Anoint Elisha the son of Shaphat of Abel-meholah as prophet in Elijah's place

Yet even though God commanded Elijah to do these three tasks, verses 19–21 only show Elijah anointing Elisha. In fact, it would be Elisha, not Elijah, who anointed Hazael and Jehu as kings (2 Kings 8:7–15; 9:1–13). Even though those commands were carried out by Elisha, it was Elijah's selection and anointing of his eventual successor that ensured the prophetic ministry, and

God's plans for it, would proceed. It was his obedience in the tiny, seemingly insignificant tasks that finally enabled him to move past his detour, to return to "normal," and to move forward.

Second, it is worth noting some facts about the prophet's mantle. The Hebrew word used for Elijah's mantle or cloak here is *adderet*. *Adderet* comes from the root word *adar*, which means "glorious" or "majestic." The mantle was covered in animal hair and would have been typically seen only on a king or a prophet. It marked the wearer as a spokesperson for God. The prophet would have very little in the way of worldly possessions and his *adderet*, literally the clothes on his back, would often be the only material good that he owned.

When Elijah found Elisha and placed the *adderet* on him, he was asking Elisha to follow him into the ministry of a prophet. We see from this action that Elijah's attitude has changed. Now, instead of desiring to die and abandoning his ministry, he is willing to invite others to follow him on the path that God has chosen for him. This shows a subtle but important change in Elijah from when he began his detour into the wilderness. His willingness to anoint Elisha shows that, even though he may not have all the answers that he wanted and his initial expectations have not been met, he now realizes that God can be trusted even if he does not know what He is doing.

Most of us will never have a detour that will end like Elijah's. We may want direction from God in the form of a memo that reads, "From the Desk of the Almighty Maker of Heaven and Earth," but God doesn't always work that way. More often than not our detours will be like falling into ditches and climbing back out. No doubt some detours will come to speedy and quick conclusions, but those will probably be the exceptions, not the rule. Still, there is much that we can learn from the last steps of the detour of one of God's mightiest prophets.

IT'S IN THE LITTLE THINGS

In 1958 the National Football League's Green Bay Packers were awful. The team had some talent, but that year they only won one game, lost ten, and tied one game. One of their defeats was a 56–0 drubbing by the team that would be the 1958 NFL champs, the Baltimore Colts. The Packers played so pathetically that Red Smith, a sportswriter from New York, remarked, "The Packers underwhelmed ten opponents, overwhelmed one, and whelmed one."[2] At the end of the worst season in franchise history, their coach of one season, Raymond "Scooter" McLean, was fired.

The Packers brought in a new coach named Vince Lombardi. Lombardi had a strict approach to the game and refused to allow his players to accept losing because of sloppiness and undisciplined play. One day as the team was practicing before the start of the season, the coach had seen enough. What happened next was a moment of pure coaching genius, described by John Eisenberg in his book *That First Season*:

> Lombardi railed at them throughout the afternoon work-out, complaining loudly about dropped passes, botched fundamentals and forgotten assignments. Obviously in a foul mood, he picked back up during a meeting that evening, telling them they had a lot to learn. Dramatically he held a ball aloft and said, "We're starting at the beginning. Gentlemen, this is a football.[3]

Imagine that. Lombardi took a group of grown men who were professional football players, eight of whom would one day make the NFL's Hall of Fame, and introduced them to a football.

What Lombardi understood about his football team was that if his team could not remember the most elementary concepts about football in practice when it was warm and they were competing against themselves, then they would never exhibit them in the bitter cold, late in games against teams like the mighty New York Football Giants. What the Packers needed to do was to take baby steps.

For the person experiencing one of life's detours, getting back to the beginning of the Christian life can be just as important as fundamentals were to the Packers in 1959. No matter the type of detour you are on, you are well served to focus on taking baby steps.

A detour is one of those times that life has gotten incredibly complicated. In fact, it is because of the complicated nature of detours that, rather than focusing on all of the things that we do not know, we instead need to focus on what we do know. Even though the thought of taking baby steps may be frustrating, we make a great mistake if we ignore them. Just as I had to take baby steps to learn to walk again after my knee surgery, focusing on some spiritual baby steps will help you to counter the feeling that your life is a downward spiral. Consider these steps:

It Is Okay to Not Know What to Do Next

Some people do better at not knowing what is coming than others. These people feel that life is best made up as they go along, and they roll with the punches. They make changes to their flight as they drive to the airport and see major change as challenges to overcome. They seem to glide through life, and at least to all appearances they take what life may throw at them smoothly and carefree. Then there are those who like to have life planned out almost to the second. These are the people who have a day planner, a calendar on their phone, a calendar on their computer, and a to-do list with a top entry of making another to-do list. If these people do something that isn't on their to-do list, they put it on the list just so that they can mark it off. Yet regardless of how you approach the future and what group you are in, you can still struggle with not knowing what to do.

There is no shame or dishonor in not knowing what to do in a given situation. Many of us mistakenly believe that our lives do or should work like the lives we see on television, or that we read about in works of fiction. The characters always know what to do. They seem to almost supernaturally know who the good guys are, who the bad guys are, what the bad guys are planning, and what the good guys need to do to stop the bad guys, all in less than an hour. Unfortunately for those of us living without a script, our next step can be a lot more tough to discern. But because we are constantly bombarded with stories of people who always seem to know what to do, and because of our own pride, we struggle to admit (even to ourselves) that we don't know what to do. It is okay that we don't know what to do.

We spend a lot of time and energy bluffing people, trying to convince them that we have everything well controlled. Frankly this is one of the silliest parts of human nature. We are plagued by a disease named "pride" that all but refuses to let us shrug our shoulders and confess that we do not know what is coming or what to do about our detours. The cure for this detour-complicating disease is a simple one—realize you may not know what to do next and be okay with it. As the philosopher

Socrates said, "True knowledge exists in knowing that you know nothing."[4]

Keep It Simple

Kelly Johnson is a legend in the aeronautic industry. He designed the P-38 Lightning, one of the Allies' most devastating planes in World War II. He was the first team leader of Lockheed Martin's famed "Skunk Works," the nickname given to the program that developed many of America's most important and famous aircraft of the last few decades. He created or supervised the design and construction of forty aircraft models including the F-80 Shooting Star (the United States' first operational jet fighter), the U-2 spy plane, the SR-71 Blackbird, and the F117A Nighthawk stealth fighter.

His work in this industry is legendary, but what Kelly Johnson may be best known for is his ability to organize and synthesize information from complicated and technical projects. Johnson often asked his engineers to make sophisticated aircraft that could be repaired by the average airplane mechanic in battlefield conditions. His summary of what was needed to do this was to, "K.I.S.S.—Keep It Simple Stupid."[5] That acronym guided Johnson and his team as they created some of the greatest airplanes that have ever been conceived.

It is the nature of the person on a detour to become inward focused. This is why isolation is such a strong temptation—you are in the midst of a problem that is threatening to overwhelm you and as a result your focus naturally drifts to you. This is okay to a point, but if your focus stays on you and never leaves, that can become a problem. One baby step to take to counteract the effects of a detour is to simply do what you know to do. Don't let your lack of knowing what to do about complex issues keep you from accomplishing the small things that you know to do.

In the Bible, Daniel continued to do what he knew to do when a law was passed that made prayer to anyone but the king illegal. Do we see him considering how to change the law? Did he file a motion against those that supported the law? Did he call lobbyists and other influential people? He might have done some of these things—the Bible does not tell us—but what we do know is that he continued to pray as he always had. Often, particularly as children, we read this story and focus on Daniel's survival in the lions' den later in the story, but there is pure spiritual brilliance in Daniel knowing that no solution apart from continuing his relationship with God would suffice. In the absence of knowing what to do, simply do what you know to do.

The simplicity that Kelly Johnson strove for in his airplane designs can be a wonderful example for dealing with detours. We can become so focused on the complex issues we are facing (or even might face) that we ignore simple actions that we know to do. This book has already discussed the invaluable role that Bible study, prayer, and other believers play in our lives, but they are so important to surviving a detour that their necessity bears repeating.

Now the answer to everyone's problems may not be to simply read the Bible and pray. Some people's detours will require them to seek serious medical, spiritual, and psychological help. Over the years a great disservice has been done to the body of Christ by those whose answer to every problem is always "just read your Bible and pray more." I am not suggesting that the answer to your cancer, to your unemployment, or to your separation doesn't involve reading your Bible and praying more. I am suggesting that when your detour threatens to drown you, maintaining these simple disciplines might keep you treading water, which is a whole lot better than drowning when you think about it.

Small Actions Can Have a Big Impact

To Elijah, throwing his mantle over Elisha might have seemed like a small act. Surely he understood the significance that he would no longer have to undertake his prophetic ministry alone; at the very least he would have someone to share the burden of the office that he occupied. But we cannot forget that of the three tasks that God gave Elijah to do, two of them would be accomplished by his protégé Elisha. What, at the time, may have seemed a small task ended up having a pretty big impact.

When you are on a detour, part of the reason that you ignore the simple things in favor of thinking and worrying about more complex issues is that you think the small tasks are too insignificant to make a difference. Elijah may have thought that bringing Elisha along as his eventual successor was minor when compared with the rampant sin and idolatry that he was fighting in Israel. There is no way that he could have known that his ministry, extended through Elisha, would continue to be powerful and far-reaching.

When you are on a detour, you are consumed by the present, and rightfully so. You face challenges and obstacles that at the very least threaten to derail what you had envisioned for the future. To you, anything you do that does not bring your detour to a safe and secure end can be seen as failure, but that is faulty reasoning. The little things that you continue to do right can pay off in a big way over time. Just the same, the little habits you pick up that you should not can become large thorns in your side as they continue. Using your detour as an excuse to do what you would not do ordinarily means that one day you will want to stop those habits but they will have gained a foothold in your life.

The entrance of Elisha into Elijah's life seemed to be a small thing at first, but years after Elijah's death, Elisha, the product of the mighty prophet's detour, would be carrying on his ministry, and the nation of Israel would still have a voice urging them to follow God and repent from their sins. It is helpful for us to remember that on Elijah's detour, when he did not know what to do, God was in the process of working out a plan for the present and the future of both the prophet and the nation of Israel. Our detours are often the same way. In those moments when we do not know what to do, God may very well be working out His plan for our benefit, and even for the benefit of those around us.

QUESTIONS FOR DISCUSSION

1. What is your typical response to a situation where you do not know what to do?
2. Who do you go to when you do not know what to do?
3. Why do we not like to admit that we don't know what to do in some situations?
4. What does it tell us about God that He so often allows us to be in circumstances in which we do not know what to do?

TEN

DETOURS AND GETTING A GLIMPSE OF GOD

1 Kings 19:11–13

I did not read H. G. Bissinger's book, *Friday Night Lights*, until I was in my mid-twenties. By that time the events described in the book were a decade and a half in the past. When I finally read the book, I found it interesting for many reasons, not the least of which was that I grew up in the town the book describes, Odessa, Texas, and I remembered many of the people and events described in the book. One event in the book struck me immediately—the visit of then vice president and presidential hopeful George H. W. Bush to the Midland-Odessa area in 1988. Here is how Bissinger describes the scene:

> The Lee and Midland high bands broke into "Deep in the Heart of Texas." Bush, wearing a blue suit, stepped off the plane onto the gangplank and for the briefest of moments looked like Notre Dame coach Lou Holtz

coming home after leading the Irish to a national championship. He started waving. In return, all the little American flags and the handmade signs started bobbing up and down.[1]

In a book about a high school football team, this passage about soon-to-be President Bush's visit to a hanger at the Midland International Airport stuck out to me for a simple reason: I was there that day. My dad, who was the principal of the small Christian school that I attended, decided that students should attend the rally. So we put down our books and pencils and scratch paper and loaded up into several white vans for the twenty-minute drive to the airport. When we arrived, everyone piled out of the vans in our school uniforms (which entailed various combinations of blue, gray, yellow, and khaki). This time, my dad's chronic earliness paid off and we all got plum spots in front of the gathering crowd.

My friends and I, all between the ages of nine and twelve, pressed forward, elbowing one another to get in front and staring wide-eyed at police officers who were close enough that we could almost reach out and touch their pistols. The event was better than any Social Studies class or curriculum that day. We were able to see and, in a way, participate in a moment of history. We heard the vice president's speech, and then excitement began to build in the crowd. The future president's wife was making her way along the rope that separated us common folk from the celebrities signing autographs.

At eleven years old I am fairly certain that I did not even know that Mrs. Bush's name was Barbara. I just knew that there was a good chance that she was going to be the First Lady of our country. The jostling and elbowing continued as we angled to get an autograph. (We did this despite only being able to name Abigail Adams and Martha Washington as previous first ladies, and most of us probably thought Martha Washington had something to do with candy.) I was one of the lucky few who got an autograph as Mrs. Bush passed by. The autograph was written on a business card–sized piece of paper and I was sure that I would treasure it always. In truth, it was probably lost before I went to sleep that night.

Not long after the future First Lady came by, another murmur began sweeping the crowd—Vice President Bush himself was making his way along the rope shaking hands and meeting folks. If the competition to be in front to get Mrs. Bush's autograph had been fierce, then the opportunity to shake the hand of the man that could be the forty-first president of the United States had the potential to be an all-out war. We jockeyed for position, somehow without drawing the curiosity and ire of the Secret Service agents in attendance. We craned our necks around those beside us, looking for the vice president, to the point that our navy blue clip-on ties threatened to choke us. Eventually he made his way to us and each one of us got to shake his hand. We all held out our hands half-expecting him to skip over us, and after we shook his hand we pulled our hands back staring at them, shocked that we had touched a vice president.

After the rally was over we made our way back to the white vans and returned to classrooms, multiplication tables, and everyday life. More than one of us proclaimed loudly on the trip that we were never going to wash the hand that the soon-to-be president shook (hopefully none of us have kept that two-decades-old pledge).

For little boys in West Texas, this seemed as close to greatness as we would ever come. I mean, come on, we were living in Odessa, Texas, for crying out loud. Most of the country could not find our city on a map, and if it was not for a book about how insane our town was about high school football, no one would have ever heard of us. We, of all people, had shaken the hand of the president. Of course, Mr. Bush probably shook hundreds of thousands of little boy's hands that campaign, but we did not care. We had gotten a glimpse of a president, and he had shaken *our* hands.

Our trip with Elijah has seen his highs and lows, mainly lows, but as you probably recall, we skipped a few verses. Now at the end of our trip with this all-too-human of prophets, it is time to examine the verses we have not considered thus far in 1 Kings 19, verses 11–13.

So He said, "Go forth and stand on the mountain before the Lord." And behold, the Lord was passing by! And a great and strong wind was rending the mountains and breaking in pieces the rocks before the Lord; but the Lord was not in the wind. And after the wind an earthquake, but the Lord was not in the earthquake. After the earthquake a fire, but the Lord was not in the fire; and after the fire a sound of a gentle blowing. When Elijah heard it, he wrapped his face in his mantle and went out and stood in the entrance of the cave. And behold, a voice came to him and said, "What are you doing here, Elijah?"

It may have seemed odd for us to have skipped these verses earlier, but rest assured there was a method to the madness. At first glance, 1 Kings 19 reads just like any other story. It has a beginning, characters, a climax, and a resolution. To those of us who grew up reading English literature, it all seems simple and straightforward. The Old Testament, however, was not written in English; it was written in Hebrew. In the Hebrew language, structure is very important.

One Hebrew literary structure is a chiasm. A chiasm is known as such because it is structured like half of the letter X (the Greek letter *chi*). Today we might think of it as structured like an Oreo cookie with the most important part, the stuffing, in the middle. In a chiasm the first part of the passage and the last part of the passage are parallels with the most important part of the passage in the middle. First Kings 19 is a chiasm. Picture the structure of 1 Kings 19 like this:

Verses 1–4   Elijah flees
  Verses 5–9a   Elijah is told to arise and eat in order
        to journey to Horeb
    Verses 9b–10   Elijah is asked, "What are you
          doing here?" and answers
      Verse 11a   Elijah is told to go out and stand
        Verses 11b–12   Elijah glimpses God
      Verse 13a   Elijah goes out and stands
    Verses 13b–14   Elijah is asked, "What are you
          doing here?" and answers
  Verses 15–18   Elijah is told to go back the way
      he came
Verses 19–21   Elijah returns

As twenty-first century Americans, a structure like this is foreign to us. The phrase "Save the best for last" is more familiar. Aside from those few deranged—or wise, depending on your view—souls who eat dessert first, most of us expect meals, life, and stories to get better and more important as they go along. Popular novels and movies place the climax, the most important part, at the end of the story, which is where we expect it, but the ancient Hebrews thought differently. A chiasm, structured as it is like an Oreo cookie, places the climax, or the story's hinge concept, right in the middle. Since these verses regarding Elijah's "face-to-face" meeting with God are the pivotal point of Elijah's detour, we will discuss them here at the end of our journey with the prophet.

In these verses, God, who has appeared somewhat elusive throughout Elijah's detour, finally shows up, or at least that is how it seems to us. All along this detour Elijah (and you and I) have continually asked the question, "Where is God?" God has, to all appearances, been out to lunch, on a vacation, or has hung a "Do Not Disturb" sign on heaven's golden gates.

There is much irony in God's "disappearance" for much of chapter 19 of 1 Kings. In chapter 18, when Elijah confronts the idolatrous prophets of Baal, he taunts the prophets and their false god by saying, "Call out with a loud voice, for he is a god; either he is occupied or gone aside, or is on a journey, or perhaps he is asleep and needs to be awakened" (v. 27). This taunt is even more antagonistic when you learn that Elijah's suggestion that Baal was "occupied" was literally the idea that the deity Baal was in the midst of relieving himself. Think of that. Elijah was so bold as to attribute the false god Baal's inactivity to a potty break. Now just weeks later Elijah has been rocked by God's seeming inactivity. He has seen God send fire from heaven, but God hasn't ended Elijah's detour. However, Elijah is about to see God in a whole new light.

GOD SHOWS UP

God has already asked Elijah what he is doing there, and he has heard Elijah's selfish, perspective-lacking complaint that the people are wicked, and that he alone is a follower of the one true God. God does not choose to argue with Elijah. He does not set up a projector and a screen to show Elijah bar graphs about how many true followers of Him there are, at least not yet. He does not give a great and eloquent speech in an attempt to show Elijah the error of his ways. God simply shows up in all of His mighty power and majesty. God's appearance to Elijah is announced by three events that even today we refer to as "acts of God."

First, there was a mighty wind. A wind so mighty that the mountains trembled and rocks were shattered by its force. It is safe to say that not even I could have slept through this wind. Often in the world of Elijah and the ancient Israelites, wind accompanied other phenomena that showed God's power and presence. In fact, this is not the first powerful wind that Elijah has felt. In 1 Kings 18:44–45, when God finally sends rain after three years of drought, along with the rain "the sky grew black with clouds and wind."

Second, there was an earthquake. Earthquakes in the Bible frequently accompany the presence of God (Psalm 114:7), and often His judgment (Psalm 18:7). There was also an earthquake when the children of Israel first gathered at Sinai (Exodus 19:18). Later, an earthquake accompanied the death of Jesus on the cross (Matthew 27:51).

Third, there was a fire. Fire was often a way in which God revealed himself and got His people's attention in the Old Testament. God revealed himself to Moses in a burning bush (Exodus 3), the children of Israel followed a pillar of fire through the desert at night (Exodus 13:17–22), and when Moses was on Mount Sinai, the mountain itself was on fire (Deuteronomy 4:11–12; 5:24–25).

Despite their frequent uses by God, all three of these powerful events had one thing in common: in this particular instance, God was not in them. Up until now Elijah served God and struggled against those who would serve idols because he knew and believed God to be mighty and powerful, the being who sent fire from heaven. That was certainly God, but God is not restricted to use such means, nor does He often choose spiritual shock and awe. As one student of the life of Elijah put it, "It was not new boldness that Yahweh gave Elijah at Horeb, but a new insight into Yahweh's way ('the voice of a gentle stillness,' 1 Kings 19:12)."[2]

It is often true for us, as it was for Elijah, that when we get a glimpse of God it is not at all what we expected. In the Scriptures God consistently does the opposite of what we think He will do. His solution to sin was not to destroy humanity and start all over, but to send his Son to take on our sin for us (2 Corinthians 5:21). His solution to a blaspheming giant was a shepherd with a slingshot (1 Samuel 17). His solution to thousands of starving people was one little boy with five loaves of bread and two fish (John 6:1–14). We must realize that who God is, is someone altogether different than who we expect Him to be.

And isn't that one of the ultimate lessons of a detour? We interact with God frequently as if He is who we want Him to be. We ignore Him for long stretches at a time only to attempt to summon His power when we need a close parking spot or something more important. While we might not think about it this way, many of us treat God as if He were a heavenly slot machine. Yet, the truth is that God is the Creator and we are the created. As Romans 9:21 says, "When a potter makes jars out of clay, doesn't he have a right to use the same lump of clay to make one jar for decoration and another to throw garbage into?" (NLT). We all want to be flowerpots, but if a detour threatens to turn us into garbage cans, or at least makes us feel that way, we find it inconceivable that God would allow such a thing to happen to us. Elijah enjoyed serving God when He sent fire from heaven, but he had to realize that that same God allowed the wicked queen to threaten his life. The God who revealed himself to Elijah in a still, small voice was the same God who sent fire from heaven.

As we walk with God we will learn that what God has for us is best for us. As David said, "A single day in your courts is better than a thousand anywhere else! I would rather be a gatekeeper in the house of my God than live the good life in the homes of the wicked" (Psalm 84:10 NLT). God's assignment for us right now may be as "gatekeepers." This realization leads us to the most fundamental concept of Christian faith—trusting God. We must trust that God is using us as trash cans rather than flowerpots for His purposes and that He can make all things right in the end. When Elijah, like David, finally embraced the still, small voice *and* the fire from heaven, he then discovered that who God is, is so much better than who he wanted Him to be in the first place.

After the wind and earthquake and fire, Elijah stepped to the edge of the cave and covered his face in his mantle, the same mantle that he would soon throw on Elisha, his eventual successor. Maybe as he stepped to the edge of the cave he even put his sandals in the same spot that Moses put his sandals in Exodus 33:18–23. There at the edge of the cave, God would repeat his question to the prophet, "What are you doing here?"

This interaction between Moses and Elijah, in spite of its obvious importance, is in some ways difficult to understand. The passage is certainly ambiguous in some areas:

- Why did God ask Elijah the same question twice?
- Why did Elijah answer the question the same way twice? Did he fail to learn anything from his detour?
- Was Elisha brought on the scene to help Elijah, or to replace him because he had failed?
- What exactly was the method that God used to reveal himself to Elijah? The phrase translated "a gentle blowing" by the NASB has at times been rendered as "a gentle whisper" (NIV), a "still small voice" (NKJV, KJV), and "a roaring and thunderous voice."[3]

These questions are all good ones to ask, and they play important roles in our understanding of the passage, but do not let unanswered questions make you lose sight of what we do know about these verses. Though Elijah did not "see" God physically, this is the moment on his detour when Elijah finally glimpsed the Almighty, and that was what was so important for Elijah. As one scholar describes Elijah, "He hears His 'still small voice' which Yahweh vouchsafes to Elijah alone, indicating his affirmation of him and his repudiation of the prophet's resignation."[4] This vision of God is intended to have a profound effect on Elijah.

Now, as we have seen, the impact was not immediate. Initially Elijah seems stuck in the idea that he is some sort of spiritual Lone Ranger stemming the tide of idolatry in Israel, but it would not be much of a detour if everything just magically fixed itself, now would it? Well, it would at least be unlike almost every detour that I have experienced. Elijah's journey back, both physically and spiritually, would be a process, but the most important part of that process was getting a glimpse of who God really was and is.

The mighty wind tearing the very rocks asunder, the earthquake shaking the huge mountain as if to hurl it from its solid base, the quivering lightning that seemed to fill the air with flame, and then the sudden hush, and calm, and silence, broken only by the sound of a low and gentle voice—these were the means God used to make the prophet see that judgment and destruction do have their place in the salvation of the world, but the greatest power of all in this work is the Spirit of God silently abiding in the hearts of men.[5]

YOUR DETOUR'S MOUNT HOREB

For Elijah the moment on the mountain, when he saw God for who God was instead of for who he wanted or wished Him to be, was the most important part of Elijah's experience. For you on your detour, getting a glimpse of God may seem to be all but impossible, but it might also mean the difference between a detour that takes your life somewhere meaningful and a detour that leads you right off the edge of a cliff. Though the process of glimpsing God in your detour may be difficult at times, the result still makes the endeavor worthwhile. In fact, there is a good chance that, much like Elijah, glimpsing God may be the very purpose for your detour. With that in mind, consider these five areas to glimpse God while on your detour.

God's Timing

I have known well-meaning and spiritual people who often said something to this effect: "God will make you wait, but he will not be late." I used to believe that, but a life spent following God has led me to conclude that He will on many occasions be very, very late. If you disagree, consider the story of Lazarus in John 11. Jesus was so late to heal Lazarus that Lazarus died and his body started to decay. Lazarus's sisters Mary and Martha considered that late, and I would too. We look at life from the perspective of human beings who are bound by constraints like time, money, education, and life expectancies. God, on the other hand, is not bound by any of these things. Jesus arrives to see Lazarus four days after his death and raises him from the dead (John 11:29–44). Jesus was not late, he was right on schedule. God can show up after the game is over, the crowd has gone home, and the teams are on the bus in order to change the score so that He wins.

The desire to see God work in our timing just might afflict every one of His children. We want and need God to act, and if we are completely honest we are most interested in God acting right now, in our timing, when we feel the most pain and discomfort from our detour. We may think of God's timing like humor columnist Dave Barry's experience with customer service: "To straighten this mess out [moving to a new house], I quit doing my job (whatever that may be) and started spending my days waiting on hold for Customer Service, listening to the snappy 'lite' jazz music they play when they are not telling you how important your call is to them."[6]

Despite our resistance to it, however, waiting is good for us. Even secular researchers have discovered that there is significant benefit to the process of waiting:

> The non-behavior called "waiting" can have enormous benefits in a number of domains. Weight Watchers teaches,

for example, that waiting in between spoonfuls lowers calorie consumption. Classroom studies have shown that superior teachers wait a while before answering their own questions; if a teacher routinely fails to wait for answers, students soon learn not to bother to try to provide them . . . In my laboratory research, I've learned about the enormous benefits waiting has for creativity. When people are struggling to solve a problem, the more time they have, the more creative they become. Even long periods of inactivity are eventually followed by breakthroughs. The main challenge is to teach people to relax while "nothing" seems to be happening.[7]

God's timing is certainly not our timing, and a detour is a good opportunity to learn that this is actually a good thing. Instead of filling our calendars and lists with things to do, waiting forces us to submit to our heavenly Father's timing. In fact, waiting may be God allowing us to see His timing, and His way of telling us to synchronize our watches with His.

God's Purposes

Our timing is not the only thing that diverges from that of the Almighty. Our failure to understand, or even acknowledge, God's purposes in our lives is something that is not easily rectified. Most people do not change their perspective unless something happens that convinces them that there is a need for it. Most of us truly believe in God's purposes until things go bad. Not "can't find a parking spot at the grocery store" bad, but really bad. Hearing the word *chemo* bad, looking at a closed casket bad, a broken relationship that will never be repaired bad. Were we allowed to plan our lives, I suspect that we would never choose cancer, death, or broken relationships for ourselves or loved ones. It is at these times, then, that God's purposes override our desired purpose for life. I would prefer God's purpose for my life to be one that shows people how if you trust God you will be healthy, successful, and loved by all, but God's purpose for my life so far has been quite different.

God can and will allow detours to happen to us, and in those times we must be careful to align our purposes with His. Like a vehicle's wheels that need to be aligned from time to time to keep the car from drifting off the road, we must realize that no matter how well intentioned or how earnest we are, life can carry us away from God's purposes if we are not intentional about aligning ourselves with them (Hebrews 2:1). Messages from the world constantly bombard us and threaten to take us far off course from God's purposes for our lives. One of God's most efficient and notable means for bringing us back to focusing on His purposes is the detour.

The switch from focusing on God's purposes for our lives to focusing on our own purposes often happens slowly. Like an airplane that is only slightly off course, we can drift almost imperceptibly into a life that is so focused on our plans and fulfilling our own desires that we don't realize how off course we are or how long we've been drifting. Detours are a time to rectify that drift and to focus on God's purposes for our lives. Trying to see God's purposes reminds us that we are not in charge of the journey or the destination.

God's Grace

Over and over again as I read 1 Kings 19 I was amazed at how surprisingly gentle and caring God seemed to be with His wayward prophet. On many occasions, just when I was sure that God was about to knock Elijah around, or maybe send a fireball from heaven to consume this previously unconquerable champion of righteousness, He does just the opposite. Many of us live our lives punishing others who disappoint us and being punished by those we disappoint, so we assume that this is how God works too. If Elijah's detour showed him, and as a result us, anything about God, it is that God is ever gracious, even when we fail Him. As one student of Elijah's detour said, "It is not difficult to believe that God loves us when, like Elijah at Cherith and on Carmel, we do His commandments, hearkening unto the voice of His word; but it is not so easy when, like Elijah in the desert, we lie stranded."[8] It is not always easy for us to believe that we are loved, but God tells us that this indeed is the truth.

The guilt and regret that accompany a detour are often worse than the detour itself. You continue to replay in your mind the events that lead to your entrance on this unwelcome path. Over and over again you second-guess yourself, and as your detour continues, you reconsider actions that you have made since the detour started that you think might have put an end to your misery. This cycle can go on and on because regret is self-perpetuating. When life has taken an unexpected turn, every day will bring a new opportunity for regret and wondering what might have been. What is so easy to forget is that without those unexpected turns you might never have seen God's grace at such depths.

God's Sovereignty

In a detour when we feel like everything is spinning out of control, we can easily assume that our feelings accurately correspond to reality. However, in spite of our feelings, one of the most important lessons that God wants to teach us in a detour is that He has been surprised by nothing that surprised us, and He is most definitely in control. When life is good we lose sight of God's sovereignty because we seem to have things under control ourselves, and when things are not going our way we lose sight of God's sovereignty because our vision is clouded with fear and doubt. This is why a detour is the perfect time to get a glimpse of God's sovereignty.

In a detour we quickly become unsure of ourselves and our decisions, and getting a glimpse of God's sovereignty takes care of all that. Consider the words of Charles Haddon Spurgeon: "Alterations and afterthoughts belong to short-sighted beings who meet with unexpected events which operate upon them to change their minds, but the Lord who sees everything from the beginning has no such reason for shifting his ground."[9] Trusting in God's sovereignty does not mean that life will always turn out as we desire, but it does mean that life will always turn out as God desires for us. On a detour, trusting in God's sovereignty is much more an act of the will than when life seems to be on track. But if you will let it, a detour will give you a glimpse of God's sovereignty in ways you never could have imagined.

On one detour that my wife and I were on, I found myself out of work. It was at this same time that we got pregnant. Not long after we learned about the pregnancy, my wife began to experience complications. The doctor did everything she could, but she told us one night that the situation did not look good and that we needed to come in the next day for a sonogram. Though she did not explicitly say it until later, the doctor—and my wife and I—anticipated the sonogram confirming that we had miscarried.

A long and largely sleepless night preceded our visit to the doctor's office the next morning. We entered the room fully prepared for the sonogram to reveal the worst. The nurse began the procedure and suddenly instead of silence we heard, *thump thump, thump thump, thump thump.* Our little son's heart was beating away. Over the next few weeks his health was touch and go. We went to numerous sonograms and doctor visits before we were finally considered to be proceeding with a "normal" pregnancy (whatever that is).

My unemployment was long and stressful, and the experience was largely a negative one. There was, however, a moment when I realized that my old job would have never let me take time off for all of the doctor appointments that were required for my wife and unborn son. Even though I would much rather have had a job all along, the detour of my unemployment allowed me to be at every doctor's visit with my pregnant wife.

Not long after the doctor appointments became less frequent I got a new job with a boss who was more than happy to let me take time off for doctor's appointments and sonograms, and to care for my son when he was born. God, in His sovereignty, knew that my being with my wife during some stressful and trying times was more important than me keeping my job.

God's Faithfulness

Most of the time on a detour you feel like there is little that you can do to change your situation. You feel powerless, and despite your best efforts, you seem unable to make any decision that would change your situation. The irony is that despite feeling that you lack choices, you must choose to believe certain things about God. One of the things that you must choose to believe in is God's faithfulness.

The Father will be faithful to His children. This concept is repeated over and over again throughout the Scriptures:

- "Kings will see and arise, princes will also bow down, because of the Lord who is faithful" (Isaiah 49:7).
- "God is faithful, through whom you were called into fellowship with His Son, Jesus Christ our Lord" (1 Corinthians 1:9).
- "Faithful is He who calls you, and He also will bring it to pass" (1 Thessalonians 5:24).
- "The Lord's lovingkindnesses indeed never cease, for His compassions never fail. They are new every morning; great is Your faithfulness" (Lamentations 3:22–23).
- "Lovingkindness will be built up forever; in the heavens You will establish Your faithfulness" (Psalm 89:2).
- "If we are faithless, He remains faithful, for He cannot deny Himself" (2 Timothy 2:13).
- "Your lovingkindness, O Lord, extends to the heavens, Your faithfulness reaches to the skies" (Psalm 36:5).
- "Your faithfulness continues throughout all generations; You established the earth, and it stands" (Psalm 119:90).
- "O Lord, You are my God; I will exalt You, I will give thanks to Your name; for You have worked wonders, plans formed long ago, with perfect faithfulness" (Isaiah 25:1).

- "Know therefore that the Lord your God, He is God, the faithful God, who keeps His covenant and His lovingkindness to a thousandth generation with those who love Him and keep His commandments" (Deuteronomy 7:9).
- "The Lord is faithful, and He will strengthen and protect you from the evil one" (2 Thessalonians 3:3).
- "Therefore, those also who suffer according to the will of God shall entrust their souls to a faithful Creator in doing what is right" (1 Peter 4:19).

No matter how circumstances may make you feel, no matter what doubts may creep into your mind, and no matter how bad things get, you can and must get a glimpse of God's faithfulness, and without a detour you might not have that opportunity. If you never found yourself in trouble, you would never be able to see God prove himself faithful and capable in your life. Seeing God's faithfulness just may be the reason your detour began in the first place.

Life has its ups and downs. One day life will be going smoothly, and the next you will be on a detour. Most of the time you will be powerless to change your circumstances, but you can control how you react to your detour and what you learn from it, even after the detour is over.

QUESTIONS FOR DISCUSSION

1. How do you feel during those times when God seems distant?
2. Why doesn't God immediately come to our rescue on detours?

3. What does it tell us about ourselves that it often takes a detour for us to get a glimpse of who God is?

4. What does it tell us about God that despite all of Elijah's issues, God still gives Elijah a glimpse of himself that few others have had?

ELEVEN

REDEEMING THE DETOUR

I never intended to write this book. To be honest, the list of books that I want to write has grown very long over the last few years, but at no point has this book ever appeared on that list. That is, until God sent my little family on a detour.

At the time that our detour started the economy was bad, my job status was shaky, and my wife and I had been trying for several months to have a baby with no success—and then the detour really began. In a span of two weeks I was let go at my job and we suffered a miscarriage. At first we endured these steps into our detour bravely, but as the months dragged on with little money, no job, and more negative pregnancy tests, "black clouds draped the heavens and crashes of thunder shook the earth" for us just as they did with Elijah.[1]

A few months into our detour I was asked by the regular teacher of the adult fellowship class at our church to fill in one Sunday when he would be out of town, and I agreed to take on the assignment. As a general rule I like teaching. I like teaching the Bible, and I have never had any trouble coming up with a topic to teach on, at least not until this particular time. Even though I had two weeks' notice that I would be teaching, I struggled mightily to come up with a topic for my lesson.

Since I was still unemployed and my wife was working full-time, I tried to help out around the house by doing a couple of projects every day, but I stopped doing projects to figure out what to teach. Despite spending every day studying, nothing seemed to come together for me. After this inability to prepare a lesson or do the dishes had gone on for over a week, I took my wife to lunch one day and the two of us quickly got into an argument. She could not understand why I was not doing what I had agreed to do around the house, and when I told her that I had spent all of my time trying to come up with something to teach, she did not understand how I could have spent all that time studying with nothing to show for it.

I had no answer for her. I spent almost all day every day looking for a job and trying to get a lesson ready, and I had come up completely empty in both pursuits. The argument between my wife and I continued until finally, in a moment of complete exasperation, I looked at my wife and confessed, "I don't know what to teach. I don't know what to do. I am just lost." After a few thoughtful moments, my lovely bride said to me, "Well, why don't you just teach on that? I bet you aren't the only one who feels that way." Though I would not admit it until a few days later, my wife had succinctly summarized the situation—we felt like life had taken a wrong turn, and we were on a long and winding detour with no end in sight.

That day I went home and returned to my studying. My wife's comment had given me an idea, and I set about getting to know my soon-to-be best friend Elijah. I turned to 1 Kings 19 and began to read about the famous and powerful prophet whose life also took a detour. That study session turned into a lesson for the Lifebuilders class at Stonebriar Community Church, and then it became this book.

One of the most fascinating things to me about Elijah is the prophet's post-detour life. Theologians and scholars have long debated the impact that Elijah's detour had on the rest of his life. Some feel that his life and ministry were affected negatively, such as F. B. Meyer, who declares that, had Elijah not run when Jezebel threatened his life,

> His own character would have escaped a stain which has resisted the obliterating erasure of the ages and still remains, fraught with shame and sorrow. Elijah's influence in Israel never recovered from that one false step. He missed a chance which never came again. And though God, in His mercy, treated him lovingly and royally as a child, He never again reinstated him as a servant in just the position which he so thoughtlessly flung away.[2]

Others, such as Chuck Swindoll, view Elijah's detour as a time of refocusing that led to an effective future ministry: "God showed Elijah that he still had a job to do—that there was still a place for him. Disillusioned and exhausted though he was, he was still God's man and God's choice for 'such a time as this' (Esther 4:14)."[3] So what exactly was Elijah's life like after his detour to the wilderness and Mount Horeb?

After descending historic Mount Horeb, Elijah returns to Israel with his new apprentice Elisha in tow, and by chapter 21 of 1 Kings he is back opposing King Ahab. From there he would continue his abrasive and confrontational reign as the most notable of God's prophets, and in the words of King Ahab, biggest "troubler" (see 18:17). Elijah again confronted wicked kings. He would once again call down fire from heaven—twice in fact (2 Kings 1:10–12). And in one of the most unique acts in all of biblical history, when it came time for the prophet to pass from the scene, rather than dying like everyone else, he was carried to heaven aboard a chariot of fire led by horses of fire. As he ascended to heaven his mantle fell to the ground and was picked up by Elisha (2 Kings 2:1–14). Say what you will about Elijah, but he certainly did not lack a flair for the dramatic.

Later in the biblical record, hundreds of years after Elijah walked the earth, the prophet Malachi tells the Israelites that they have not seen the last of this "hairy man with a leather girdle bound about his loins" (2 Kings 1:8):

> Remember the law of Moses My servant, even the statutes and ordinances which I commanded him in Horeb for all Israel. "Behold, I am going to send you Elijah the prophet before the coming of the great and terrible day of the Lord. He will restore the hearts of the fathers to their children and the hearts of the children to their fathers, so that I will not come and smite the land with a curse." (4:4–6)

After the prophecy in Malachi, Elijah appeared again, this time not in a prophecy but in person on an unnamed mountain (Mark 9:2–8). Both Moses and Elijah appeared and talked with Jesus not long before Christ's death, burial, and resurrection. While on the mountain the voice of God the Father announced, "This is My beloved Son." The scene of Jesus conversing with the long-dead Moses and the prophet who disappeared in a chariot of fire was witnessed by three of Jesus' disciples: Peter, James, and John, and is known to most students of the Bible as the "transfiguration." Not one of the three disciples gives any indication as to the conversation between the Son of God and two of the most prominent of Old Testament Israelites. There for a few brief moments, however, the mighty prophet was back on another mountain.

After the transfiguration, Elijah is mentioned by the apostle Paul as an example of God's faithfulness in Romans 11. He is then mentioned in the book of James where it is said of Elijah:

> *Elijah was a man with a nature like ours, and he prayed earnestly that it would not rain, and it did not rain on the earth for three years and six months. Then he prayed again, and the sky poured rain and the earth produced its fruit.* *(5:17–18)*

This last specific mention of Elijah in the Scriptures is a significant one in that James gives Elijah an everyman quality that we do not typically ascribe to this prophet. Most of us have never been described as "hairy . . . with a leather girdle bound about [our] loins." I am also confident that the percentage of us who have successfully called down fire from heaven is fairly small (somewhere around zero). Further, I assume that most, and by most I mean all, of the readers of this book have never taken a ride to heaven in a fiery chariot. Elijah is a lot of things, but an average man he most certainly is not. That is why it is so surprising that James asserts that Elijah was just another one of the common folk.

James's statement goes further than saying that Elijah was similar to us, he says that we are made of the same substance. The word translated as "nature" is the Greek word *homoiopathes*, which is used of objects that are of the same kind or quality. This passage in James says that all of us, detours and all, are the same or identical to the great Elijah. As Charles Haddon Spurgeon said of this passage and this prophet,

> Now as Elias [Elijah] was a man of like passions with us, we may conclude that the way in which God dealt with him is very much the way in which he would deal with us. With a similar case, and the same physician, we may look for the same treatment. As, therefore, the Lord spake to Elijah not by earthquake, nor wind, nor fire, but by the still small voice, so in all probability will he speak to us.[4]

Some theologians, particularly those who study prophesied future events, suggest that Elijah's work on earth may not be done. Halfway through the book of Revelation the apostle John relates coming events revolving around two witnesses that will stand for God in the midst of the Great Tribulation:

> *If anyone wants to harm them, fire flows out of their mouth and devours their enemies; so if anyone wants to harm them, he must be killed in this way. These have the power to shut up the sky, so that rain will not fall during the days of their prophesying; and they have power over the waters to turn them into blood, and to strike the earth with every plague, as often as they desire. (11:5–6)*

These two witnesses are not specifically identified in the book of Revelation, but because of their actions such as calling down fire, preventing rain, turning water into blood, and bringing plagues upon the earth, many have asserted that the identities of these two mysterious and powerful witnesses are no less than

Moses and Elijah. Calling down fire from heaven and having the power to proclaim a drought certainly sound like the pre- and post-detour life of our friend Elijah, though the Scriptures do not give us the identity of either witness.

The life of the great prophet, his detour, and his life after his detour are important to us because we are just like Elijah. We may not believe that we are made of the same stuff that Elijah was, but we are. We may believe that our detour has completely derailed our lives, but more than likely one day we will look back like Elijah and realize that that was not the case at all. As our journey with Elijah comes to a close, we will consider a question as a way of concluding our journey: How do we recover from our detours?

To begin answering this question, let me make three statements that will provide direction. First, you will experience detours in your life. Second, you may or not may not know God's purpose for your detour. Third, no matter what your detour is, or the effect it has on your life, life will go on.

Think about those three concepts for a second. Detours are coming. There is nothing that you can do about it. From time to time life throws us curveballs that we are not expecting. And despite the fact that God is in control, He may not always feel the need to let you know what His purposes are in allowing the detour to come into your life. You might have some indication as to God's purposes, or you might not. Finally, at some point life will return to a variation of normal, whatever that is, and even if your life is forever changed, the world will keep turning. When viewed in light of these three concepts, we realize that detours are not to be just survived. Rather they are a part of life that matters, that we must prepare for, and that we must deal with when they arrive.

Given these three concepts when we encounter—and eventually leave behind—a detour, our philosophy should not be that of simple survival, but of redemption. To most of us a detour feels like failure, like a waste of time, like a massive earthquake that has shifted our lives. Still, if we change our focus—particularly in hindsight when our detour is beginning to fade in the rearview mirror—to viewing our detour through the lens of redemption, it will greatly affect how we recover from our detour and how we approach the next one.

Determining to redeem your detour can make a tremendous difference in your life. Recall that as we viewed Elijah's detour, we examined a process. Though we considered it in a slightly different order, the process was:

- Unmet expectations, followed by out-of-control emotions that led to isolation.
- Isolation gave way to negative comparisons.
- God intervened and saw to it that Elijah's personal needs were met.
- Elijah began the process of retracing his steps.
- Elijah struggled to view reality with the proper perspective, and even a glimpse of God left Elijah with an imperfect understanding of God and His plan for the life of the prophet and the nation of Israel.
- Eventually, even though he lacked understanding, Elijah acted by doing what he knew to do.

Your detour may or may not follow a similar pattern to Elijah's. You cannot control what your detour is, how it starts, how long it lasts, or when it ends. What you can control is how you react to your detour. A detour, even when it is over, can leave you bitter, disillusioned, doubtful, and distrusting—or it can grow your faith, make you stronger, and give you a greater sense of who your heavenly Father is. Based on his later use by God, it is apparent that upon reflection Elijah got more out of his detour than it may appear at first glance. For many of us our detours will work the same way. After some time has passed we just might feel differently about the experience.

After your detour is over you will need to make a choice. That choice will involve how you let the detour affect your life going forward. Will you choose to dwell on the negative and become bitter, or will you choose to allow God to bring something fruitful and productive from your experience? Will you look back on your detour with regret or will you see redemption? Redeeming your detour involves making a conscious decision to move past the negative emotions that come along with your detour, and choosing instead to view a largely negative experience as God views it. Redeeming your detour is coming to the conclusion that, even if you do not know why God allowed this to happen to you, you can learn and grow from it.

THE PLAY-DOH PRINCIPLE

Prior to your detour, you were under the impression that your life was headed in a particular direction. There is a chance that your detour will bring you back to the same road you were on when your detour started. More than likely, however, your detour will bring you to an entirely new road altogether. This is because detours are not dead ends or pit stops, but often divine redirections.

Now most of us would like to think that the best way for God to change the course of our lives would be for Him to send us an itinerary letting us know of the upcoming changes. In our minds, that would be the most effective and simplest method. The problem is that while that method would certainly be simpler, it would not increase our faith or teach us about our heavenly Father (and I wouldn't have had a book to write). If we are truly honest with ourselves, we would admit that most of us do not change our minds or submit to change willingly, and an itinerary from God would do little to correct that.

Humans are resistant to change, even when change would make a great deal of sense. In one of the almost infinite number of articles that instruct business managers and supervisors on how to lead their employees to change, organizational psychologists Robert Kegan and Lisa Laskow Lahey say that some people have "a kind of personal immunity to change."[5] This is why the Play-Doh principle is so important.

In 1927 Kutol Products of Cincinnati, Ohio, began marketing a new cleaning substance called Kutol Wall Cleaner.[6] The doughy, claylike substance was composed of flour, water, salt, boric acid, and silicone oil. At the time most homes in America were heated by coal furnaces, which were more efficient and cost-effective than wood-burning stoves. The downside to coal stoves was that they tended to leave a sooty, messy residue on walls that was difficult to clean. This is where Kutol Wall Cleaner came in. It became a hot seller because it was one of the few cleaners that could effectively clean wallpaper and flat-paneled walls.

For two decades Kutol Products produced cardboard can after cardboard can of wallpaper cleaner to the delight of housewives across the country, and the company's owner, Cleo McVicker. The late 1940s, however, saw Kutol Products and their wall cleaner steaming toward a detour. First, the need for wallpaper cleaner was dramatically reduced after World War II as furnaces powered by oil and gas were introduced and rapidly gained in popularity. Then in 1949 Cleo McVicker, the company's heart and soul, died in an airplane crash. Cleo's widow, Irma, inherited the company and quickly placed her son Joe in a prominent position in the company, hoping that he would be able to turn the company around with the help of his brother-in-law. Then Joe found out that, at twenty-five years of age, he had a rare form of cancer. Joe went to New York to have surgery to remove his cancer, but the surgery was unsuccessful. He was sent back to Cincinnati with the doctors having reached the end of their expertise. He and his company both looked to be dying a slow, painful death. The winter of 1954, as the holidays approached, Joe decided to undergo experimental radiation treatments in an attempt to save his life.

At the same time that Joe was undergoing experimental treatments in Cincinnati, his sister-in-law Kay, who lived in New Jersey, was searching for inexpensive and creative ideas to decorate her community nursery school. Purely by accident Kay happened to read that wallpaper cleaner could be used to make Christmas ornaments. She went out and purchased a can of Kutol Wall Cleaner and took it to the children in her nursery. The children used cookie cutters to make shapes and designs out of the doughy substance, and then she took their designs home and dried them in her oven. Presto! The children had unique and creative Christmas ornaments. Kay called Joe, who took a break from his radiation treatments to fly to New Jersey to see these ornaments. There, looking at a Christmas tree full of ornaments made from his failing company's cleaner, Joe and Kay realized that Kutol Wall Cleaner might not be finished after all.

Joe went back to Cincinnati. The factory kept producing the same basic substance with a few slight changes, but now instead of cranking out wall cleaner they produced buckets and buckets of a new substance that they christened Play-Doh. The factory was renamed the Fun Factory, and the "new" toy took off.[7] People no longer needed wall cleaner, but kids loved Play-Doh. The company rebounded from near extinction, and Joe even beat cancer. The detour experienced by Kutol Products gives us an important principle regarding detours: What we see as a deviation from our journey just might be God's changing of our destination.

THE BRICK PRINCIPLE

In retrospect, we see that detours are often about changing our destination, about a new place to go—that was the Play-Doh principle. Detours can also be about changing who we are. A detour can and will force you to adapt to new situations by learning new skills, developing new attitudes, and evolving as a person. It is the change in you that is the point of the Brick principle.

In the late 1970s a brick mason named Joe lived in Mississippi. Joe was a husband and the father of six boys, and he was known as one of the hardest working men around. Not only was Joe hardworking, but he demanded just as much hard labor out of his sons, who helped him lay bricks anytime they were not in school. Joe's boys would often work eight-hour shifts with their father over the summer and on the weekends. The boys stacked bricks, shoveled, slapped mortar on the bricks, and banged their knuckles. One of Joe's sons, Jerry, was a particularly hard worker, so much so that Joe would later say of his son, "He could stand more sun than I could. He handled bricks better than any worker I ever had. I was sorry to see him go."[8]

On those hot Mississippi days when Joe and his sons were laying bricks in the humid heat of the Deep South, Jerry was often placed on the top of a scaffold. His role at the top of the scaffold was to catch the bricks that were tossed up to him by his dad and brothers. Over and over again Jerry caught those bricks. In his own words, catching all those bricks taught Jerry something: "The meaning of hard work."⁹ Catching all those also taught Jerry one other thing—how to catch.

Other boys were enjoying their summers off from school doing what young boys want to do during the summer: swimming, sleeping, goofing off, and anything that is not productive. Meanwhile, young Jerry was on a detour. He showed up to work with his dad every day on the scaffold while many of his classmates had it easy. The detour of the bricks turned Jerry Rice into the football player that in 2010 the NFL Network proclaimed the greatest to ever play the game. Jerry Rice became the greatest football player due in large part to two characteristics: a tireless work ethic and hands that could catch almost any pass thrown his way.

God allows some detours to come to us to change who we are. If Jerry Rice had never had to work long days on top of a scaffold catching bricks, he might never have become the greatest player ever at catching footballs. Many times detours force us to develop abilities that we might never have had without that detour. Think of Joseph in the Old Testament. Early in Joseph's life God gave him visions of himself as a ruler, and then God proceeded to allow Joseph to go on a detour. Then his detour had a detour, and then that detour had a detour. Joseph went from the favorite son, to a slave, to a prisoner before finally ending up as the second-most powerful ruler in Egypt (Genesis 37–47). It was

God's plan for Joseph to be a ruler over Egypt all along, but it was on Joseph's detour that he learned *how* to rule. Even though you may not know it at the time of your detour, your detour may be just the thing to get you ready for what God has in store for you.

THE NEXT PRINCIPLE

In the late 1970s Steve Jobs and Steve Wozniak formed a computer company working out of Jobs's parents' garage. Together the two men built the company's first generations of computers. The company produced the Apple I (made largely out of wood), the Apple II, and the Apple III, and by the end of 1983 introduced the world to a brand new computer, the Macintosh.

In January of 1984, during the third quarter of that year's Super Bowl, Apple debuted a now famous commercial based on George Orwell's book *1984*. In Orwell's book, society is controlled via constant surveillance and mind control by a dictator from a group known as The Party. Apple's commercial showed a society of people whose technological choices were all made for them, and everyone was the same. The commercial promises that Apple computers will ensure that the year 1984 will be nothing like the book *1984*, because the Macintosh offers freedom and creativity in computing. Jobs headed the Macintosh division at Apple, and Jobs and his company looked to be on top of the world.

By the end of that year, however, the Macintosh's sales were slumping. Making matters worse for Jobs, a man he had hand-picked as the CEO of Apple had a different vision for the company than Jobs did, leading to a tremendous amount of tension in the company. A power struggle between the two men continued for several months until May of 1985 when the board of directors sided with the current CEO. Steve Jobs, the man who had cofounded the company, was removed as the director of the Macintosh division. A few months later Steve Jobs resigned: he was out at his own company.

For most people, this would have been a devastating turn of events, and it was for Steve Jobs. In disgust Jobs sold the 85,000 shares of Apple stock that he owned and moved on to other ventures. He used the money from the sale of the stocks to do two things. First, he purchased a struggling computer animation studio that later would be renamed Pixar. He gave George Lucas, the creator of *Star Wars* and *Indiana Jones*, $5 million for the company, and then invested $5 million of his own money into the company. Second, he founded another computer company named NeXT.

Under Jobs's leadership Pixar went from floundering to thriving. Pixar revolutionized animated moviemaking. Movies such as *Toy Story*, *Finding Nemo*, and *Cars* made Pixar a household name, familiar to every child—and consequently every parent. Two decades after Jobs purchased Pixar, it was sold to the Walt Disney Company for $7.4 billion. At the time of the sale Jobs still owned 50.1 percent of the company and turned a massive profit on his original investment.

Unfortunately for Jobs, NeXT was nowhere near as successful as Pixar. The mission of NeXT was to create computer workstations for higher education and business. For over a decade, NeXT produced its computers making little dent in the computer market. In 1991, six years after the company began, a writer for *Forbes Magazine* had this to say about Jobs and his company:

> Here's another view of Steve Jobs: Sculley [the manager that fired him at Apple] was right after all. Jobs is

a terrible manager. And his technological sense is not infallible: Where he had a totally free hand (in the Lisa project at Apple), he produced a failure. Now, in complete control of Next, he has made fundamentally wrong decisions that could well doom the venture. None of this is to deny Jobs the credit due him for what he did in cofounding Apple. But there are very few miracle workers in the business world, and it is now clear that Steve Jobs is not one of them.[10]

NeXT never really amounted to much, and in a strange turn of events it was purchased in 1997 by Apple, who had been struggling to sell computers themselves.[11]

The Steve Jobs who returned to Apple in 1997, and who would be named CEO in 2000, was a different man than the one who had left in disgrace over a decade earlier. As Jobs would say in his 2005 commencement address at Stanford University, "I didn't see it then, but it turned out that getting fired from Apple was the best thing that could have ever happened to me. The heaviness of being successful was replaced by the lightness of being a beginner again, less sure about everything. It freed me to enter one of the most creative periods of my life."[12] When Jobs came back to Apple, he had rediscovered what it was he loved about technology and computers.

Steve Jobs's detour gives us what we are going to call the NeXT principle, which says that we must bear in mind when reflecting on our own detours that sometimes detours serve the purpose of bringing our focus and sense of priority back to where they ought to be. As we go throughout our daily lives, many things serve to distract and occupy us. We must work jobs, pay bills, mow lawns, do dishes, feed pets, change diapers, take children to school, attend PTA meetings, and on and on the list goes. Very quickly that seemingly endless list of things to do has a way of obscuring what is truly important and worthwhile in life. What getting fired did for Steven Jobs was to remind him what it was that made him so passionate about technology in the first place.

In a detour you probably find ways to jettison thoughts and actions that will not solve your problems. You focus on getting down to business. If something does not have the ability to end your detour or solve your problem, you spend little time on it and move on to the next idea or task. This focus can be good. Yet if you are not careful, once your life has returned to normal, you will once again resume your distracted and unfocused existence. Resist this urge! The sense of desperation and focus that you experience during a detour may have been sorely lacking in your life before.

When you are on a detour you pray like you mean it. You ask God to act because you are desperate for Him to do so. You beseech the heavenly Father because you are convinced that unless He acts there is no way out of the problem in which you find yourself. Do not let this attitude go. Remain desperate. It is foolish, although typical of most of us, to end a detour and return to life as it was before. We pray and seek God inconsistently until we have a detour, then we pray and seek God feverishly during the detour. But once the darkest clouds have parted, we return to an inconsistent relationship with the Father. Steve Jobs learned that sometimes a detour can be about showing us what we are missing. He learned his lesson. Will you?

THE SCAR PRINCIPLE

It would be nice if all of life's detours operated like television shows, or at least like movies. They would have a defined start time, some breaks in the middle, and a nice, tidy ending. When you are watching a show and the good guys catch the bad guys but the show still has thirty minutes left, you know a twist is coming, but you also know that the twist has to be resolved within the next thirty minutes. Unfortunately our lives, and particularly our detours, do not operate the same way.

Even when life has returned to "normal," your detour may have changed your definition of normal. Your detour may have changed your destination, it may have changed you, it may have changed your perspective and focus, and it may have left you with something you surely did not want—scars.

Most people who see me—even the unfortunate souls who have to do so regularly—never notice the scar above my right eye. To someone who is not looking for it, the scar is almost imperceptible. It has been there since I was seventeen years old and playing basketball for my high school in the end-of-season tournament. I rebounded a missed shot and as I turned to dribble up the court, someone from the other team decided not to let a little thing like rules get in the way. An elbow came crashing into my face, narrowly missing my eye and separating me from the ball. No foul was called, they scored two points, and I had to leave the game for several minutes to try to stop the bleeding. We lost the game, and I gained a new scar.

Just like my ill-fated rebound, our detours can leave us with scars. Often we think that detours should work like that of Job, who lost everything but at the end of his story got back twice as much as what he lost (Job 42:10). When we think that way we tend to forget what Job lost. He lost ten children. Later on he would have ten more children, but ask any parent who has lost a child—you do not replace children. Job's health was restored, but a man that scraped boils off his body with broken pottery shards surely had a few reminders of just how low his life had once been. Well, maybe Job is just a bad example. What about Joseph? He had tremendous detours, but surely everything was magically better when his detours ended. Certainly at the end of his detour Joseph recovered well—not everyone can say that their detour netted them a new job as the second-in-command of the entire country. But before you assume that Joseph lived happily ever after, remember that his detour included betrayal by his brothers, slavery, a false accusation, and time in an Egyptian prison. Joseph may have come out on top, but the level of betrayal he faced and years in an Egyptian prison probably contained enough angst to send even the most stable person into therapy for a very long time.

Those who endure a detour and emerge on the other side with nothing but sunshine and roses are the exception (that is, if they actually exist). Your detour may leave you with physical scars, or they may be mental and spiritual; invisible, but no less real. God could allow you to experience bad times and then magically make it all better, but since that has not been His pattern with His saints, you will probably emerge from your detour with some scars. The Scar principle reminds us of two reasons why we have scars from our detours.

First, scars help us remember. Our passion and desperation for God can easily dissipate when the pressure is off; scars are one way to counteract that impulse. You might not want to remember your detour. You may spend a vast amount of time and energy to distract yourself from remembering what happened to you when life took a wrong turn, but God's purposes in it will do you no good if you do not remember it. If nothing else, remembering your detour will make you appreciate that you are no longer on that detour.

Second, scars help us relate. I never understood what it was like to lose a job until I lost mine. I never understood the pain of a miscarriage until it was my pain. I never understood what it was like to hear the word *cancer*, until it was my mom saying it. Whatever your detour is, you will be uniquely situated to understand those who have undergone or will undergo something similar. Your scars may exist so that you can be there for someone with scars of their own.

CONCLUSION

Some time after my adventure on Eagle Mountain Lake, I returned to my in-law's lake house and once again sat astride a WaveRunner. This time I ran it into the boat dock at a high speed, bailing just before it hit the dock. I no longer ride Wave-Runners for obvious reasons. I did not, however, get lost on the lake. You see, I know Eagle Mountain Lake pretty well, because one hot afternoon I spent time on a detour on that lake. I learned that my wife's family's house was located in Pelican Bay, that her grandparents had a place just around the bend, and I even know where a nice gentleman lives who will give you a tank of gas.

If someone were ever to be lost on that lake, I am who they should call. If you have not been in the midst of a detour while you read this book, then hang on, because another Eagle Mountain Lake with your name on it will be coming up soon. When your detours come and you find your life speeding in the wrong direction, our friend Elijah would be a good one to call. He knows all about detours—he has been there before.

QUESTIONS FOR DISCUSSION

1. How much do you struggle with anger and bitterness when God allows you to go on a detour?
2. Do you find that even years later you spend time wishing life would have taken different turns that it did?
3. What are some things that God has taught you on detours?
4. What does it tell us about God that despite the fact that it may hurt, He still uses detours in our lives?

NOTES

INTRODUCTION

1. Arthur W. Pink, *The Life of Elijah* (London: Banner of Truth Trust, 1963), p. 106.

CHAPTER 1

1. Ronald Barclay Allen, "Elijah, the Broken Prophet," *Journal of the Evangelical Theological Society* 22/3 (Sept. 1979): pp. 199–200, available online at http://www.etsjets.org/files/JETS-PDFs/22/22-3/22 -3-pp193-202_JETS.pdf.
2. D. A. Carson, *The Difficult Doctrine of the Love of God* (Wheaton, IL: Crossway, 2000), pp. 11–12.
3. We read 1 Corinthians 10:13, "No temptation has overtaken you but such as is common to man; and God is faithful, who will not allow you to be tempted beyond what you are able, but with the temptation will provide the way of escape also, so that you will be able to endure it," without often realizing that solitude is not intrinsic to the verse. Our fellow believers in Christ are an avenue of escape (if not the primary one) that God has provided for us.
4. United States Joint Forces Command, "Joint Operating Environment 2010," p. ii, available online at http://www.fas.org/man/eprint/ joe2010.pdf.

CHAPTER 2

1. The KJV, NKJV, and ASV translate this as "saw," but the NASB and ESV translate it as "was afraid." The NIV and NET both translate it as "was afraid" and include a note notifying the reader that "saw" is a possibility.

2. Jack Katz, *How Emotions Work* (Chicago: University of Chicago Press, 1999), p. 1.
3. Daniel Goleman, *Emotional Intelligence* (New York: Bantam Books, 1995), p. 9.
4. Anjana Ahuja, "The Intimate Link Between Smell and Memory," *London Times*, December 6, 2007.
5. Augustine J. Kposowa and Stephanie D'Auria, "Association of Temporal Factors and Suicides in the United States, 2000–2004," *Social Psychiatry and Psychiatric Epidemiology* 45.4 (2010): pp. 433–45.
6. Goleman, *Emotional Intelligence*, p. 6.

CHAPTER 3

1. Simon J. DeVries, *1 Kings*, Word Biblical Commentary, vol. 12 (Waco, TX: Word Books, 1985), p. 235.
2. N. L. deClaisse-Walford, "Genesis 2: 'It Is Not Good for the Human to Be Alone,'" *Review and Expositor* 103.2 (2006): p. 348.
3. Study conducted by the National Opinion Research Center at the University of Chicago; cited in "For Many, the Ties That Bind Are Falling Away," *San Francisco Chronicle*, June 24, 2006.
4. Shankar Vedantam, "Social Isolation Growing in U.S. Study Says," *Washington Post*, June 23, 2006.
5. John T. Cacioppo and William Patrick, *Loneliness: Human Nature and the Need for Social Connection* (New York: W. W. Norton & Co., 2008), p. 52.
6. R. A. Schoevers, A. T. Beekman, D. J. Deeg, M. I. Geerlings, C. Jonker, and Tilburg W. Van, "Risk Factors for Depression in Later Life," *Journal of Affective Disorders* 59.2 (2000): pp. 12–137.
7. Cacioppo and Patrick, *Loneliness*, pp. 107–108.
8. O. Ybarra, E. Burnstein, P. Winkielman, M. C. Keller, M. Manis, E. Chan, and J. Rodriguez, "Mental Exercising Through Simple Socializing: Social Interaction Promotes General Cognitive Functioning," *Personality & Social Psychology Bulletin* 34.2 (2008): pp. 248–59.
9. J. Holt-Lunstad, T. B. Smith, J. B. Layton, "Social Relationships and Mortality Risk: A Meta-Analytic Review," *Public Library of Science Medicine* 7/7 (2010), available online at http://www.plosmedicine.org/article/info:doi/10.1371/journal.pmed.1000316.

CHAPTER 4

1. Simon J. DeVries, *1 Kings*, Word Biblical Commentary, vol. 12 (Waco, TX: Word Books, 1985), p. 235.
2. Howard G. Hendricks, *Elijah: Confrontation, Conflict, and Crisis* (Chicago: Moody Press, 1972), p. 57.
3. Sam Sommers, "The Toolbox of Self-Deception, Part III," Science of Small Talk blog, *Psychology Today*, September 12, 2009, http://www.psychologytoday.com/blog/science-small-talk/200909/the-toolbox-self-deception-part-iii.
4. Sonja Lyubomirsky, "When Everyone Loses: Why Aren't We More Dejected about the Economy?" How of Happiness blog, Psychology Today, December 29, 2008, http://www.psychologytoday.com/blog/how-happiness/200812/when-everyone-loses.
5. C. S. Lewis, *Mere Christianity* (San Francisco: HarperSanFrancisco, 2001), p. 122.
6. Lydia Saad, "More Workers OK with Their Pay in 2010," Gallup, August 19, 2010, http://www.gallup.com/poll/142310/Workers-Pay-2010.aspx.
7. Marina Krakovsky, "More Workers Satisfied with Their Pay in a Worse Economy?" Secrets of the Moneylab blog, *Psychology Today*, August 24, 2010, http://www.psychologytoday.com/blog/secrets-the-moneylab/201008/more-workers-satisfied-their-pay-in-worse-economy.
8. Craig S. Keener, *The IVP Bible Background Commentary: New Testament* (Downers Grove, IL: InterVarsity Press, 1993), Logos Bible Software.
9. Ibid.
10. Lewis, *Mere Christianity*, p. 124.

CHAPTER 5

1. F. B. Meyer, *Elijah and the Secret of His Power* (London: Morgan and Scott, 1901), p. 108.
2. H. W. Brands, *TR: The Last Romantic* (New York: Basic Books, 1997), pp. 720–22.
3. Howard G. Hendricks, *Elijah: Confrontation, Conflict, and Crisis* (Chicago: Moody Press, 1972), p. 61.

4. Warren W. Wiersbe, *In Praise of Plodders!* (Grand Rapids: Kregel, 1994), p. 47.

5. "How to Get out of Quicksand," http://www.wikihow.com/Get-out -of-Quicksand (accessed April 9, 2011).

CHAPTER 6

1. John F. Walvoord and Roy B. Zuck, *The Bible Knowledge Commentary: Old Testament* (Wheaton, IL: Victor Books, 1983), 582.

2. D. Epp-Tiessen, "1 Kings 19: The Renewal of Elijah," *Direction Fresno* 35.1 (2006): p. 36.

3. Ibid.

4. Raymond B. Dillard, *Faith in the Face of Apostasy: The Gospel According to Elijah and Elisha* (Phillipsburg, NJ: P&R, 1999), pp. 53–54.

5. Ronald Barclay Allen, "Elijah, the Broken Prophet," *Journal of the Evangelical Theological Society* 22/3 (Sept. 1979): p. 201, available online at http://www.etsjets.org/files/JETS-PDFs/22/22-3/22 -3-pp193-202_JETS.pdf.

CHAPTER 7

1. Susan Paterno, "The Question Man," *American Journalism Review*, October 2000, available online at http://www.ajr.org/article.asp?id =676.

2. Howard G. Hendricks, *Elijah: Confrontation, Conflict, and Crisis* (Chicago: Moody Press, 1972), p. 57.

3. Hendricks, *Elijah*, p. 62.

4. In a 2003 article pitcher David Wells suggested the number was 25–40 percent (Associated Press, "Wells Says Amphetamine, Steroid Use Rampant in Baseball," *Sports Illustrated*, February 27, 2003, available online at http://sportsillustrated.cnn.com/baseball/news/2003/02/27/ wells_drugs_ap/) and in Jose Canseco's book *Juiced* he suggests 85 percent (New York: It Books, 2006).

5. William Booth, "Reality Is Only an Illusion, Writers Say," *Washington Post*, August 19, 2004.

6. Erin Nipper, "C.S.I. Offers False Reality," *The Lariot Online*, January 27, 2010, http://www.baylor.edu/lariat/news.php?action=story &story=68015.

7. "Clarkson Opens Up about Airbrush Controversy," *San Francisco Chronicle*, September 8, 2009, available at http://www.sfgate.com/cgi-bin/blogs/dailydish/detail?entry_id=47106#ixzz1ClULnkuB.

CHAPTER 8

1. D. Epp-Tiessen, "1 Kings 19: The Renewal of Elijah," *Direction Fresno* 35.1 (2006): p. 39.
2. Arthur W. Pink, *Elijah* (Edinburgh: Banner of Truth Trust, 1963), p. 25.
3. Patricia Sellers, "So You Fail, Now What?" *Fortune Magazine*, May 1, 1995.
4. "Thomas Edison's Predictions: Spot On," CBS News Tech Talk from January 28, 2011, http://www.cbsnews.com/8301-501465_162-20029941-501465.html.

CHAPTER 9

1. D. Epp-Tiessen, "1 Kings 19: The Renewal of Elijah," *Direction Fresno* 35.1 (2006): p. 40.
2. David Maraniss, *When Pride Still Mattered: A Life of Vince Lombardi* (New York: Simon & Schuster, 1999), p. 191.
3. John Eisenberg, *That First Season: How Vince Lombardi Took the Worst Team in the NFL and Set It on the Path to Glory* (Boston: Houghton Mifflin Harcourt, 2009), p. 102.
4. Lloyd A. Johnson, *A Toolbox for Humanity: 3000 Years of Thought* (Victoria, B.C: Trafford, 2003), p. 67.
5. Ben Rich, *Clarence Leonard "Kelly" Johnson: A Biographical Memoir* (Washington D.C.: National Academies Press, 1995).

CHAPTER 10

1. H. G. Bissinger, *Friday Night Lights* (Reading, MA: Addison-Wesley, 1990), p. 184.
2. Ronald B. Allen, "Elijah, the Broken Prophet," *Journal of the Evangelical Theological Society* 22/3 (Sept. 1979): pp. 199–200, available online at http://www.etsjets.org/files/JETS-PDFs/22/22-3/22-3-pp193-202_JETS.pdf.

3. J. Lust, "A Gentle Breeze or a Roaring Thunderous Sound? Elijah at Horeb: 1 Kings Xix 12," *Vetus Testamentum* 25.1 (1975): pp. 110–15. Lust says, "The philological analysis of 1 Kings xix 12 as well as the study of the context and the traditions involved suggest a translation . . . differing from the commonly accepted one. We propose to read: 'A roaring and thunderous voice.'"

4. Robert L. Cohn, "The Literary Logic of 1 Kings 17–19," *Journal of Biblical Literature* 101.3 (1982): p. 342.

5. Sylvester Burnham, "The Mission and Work of Elijah," *The Biblical World* 24.3 (1904): p. 184.

6. Dave Barry, "100 Years of Solitude, Waiting for Customer Service," *Miami Herald*, November 5, 2000.

7. Robert Epstein, "Waiting," Psychology Today, September 1, 2001, http://www.psychologytoday.com/articles/200109/waiting.

8. F. B. Meyer, *Elijah and the Secret of His Power* (London: Morgan and Scott, 1901), p. 110.

9. C. H. Spurgeon, *Psalms* (Wheaton, IL: Crossway, 1993), p. 16.

CHAPTER 11

1. Arthur W. Pink, *The Life of Elijah* (London: Banner of Truth Trust, 1963), p. 106.

2. F. B. Meyer, *Elijah and the Secret of His Power* (London: Morgan and Scott, 1901), pp. 100–101.

3. Charles R. Swindoll, *Elijah: A Man of Heroism and Humility* (Nashville: Word, 2000), p. 120.

4. Charles Haddon Spurgeon, "God's Gentle Power," sermon delivered at the Metropolitan Tabernacle, Newington, England, September 10, 1871, available at http://www.spurgeon.org/sermons/3498.htm.

5. Robert Kegan and Lisa L. Lahey, "The Real Reason People Won't Change," *Harvard Business Review* 79.10 (2001): 84.

6. Tim Walsh, *Timeless Toys: Classic Toys and the Playmakers Who Created Them* (Kansas City, MO: Andrews McMeel, 2005), pp. 115–20.

7. Avery Yale Kamila, "Oh Happy Clay," *Portland Press Herald*, November 14, 2010.

8. Rick Telander, "Let's Hand It to Him," *Sports Illustrated*, December 26, 1994.

9. Ralph Wiley, "Rice Is a Breed Apart," *Sports Illustrated*, September 28, 1987.

10. Julie Pitta, "The Steven Jobs Reality Distortion Field," *Forbes Magazine*, April 29, 1991.

11. Eventually NeXT would be used by Apple as the basis for their popular OSX operating system. Some of the computing principles first developed for NeXT are still in use on the Internet today.

12. Steve Jobs, Stanford University Commencement Address, June 12, 2005.

NOTE TO THE READER

The publisher invites you to share your response to the message of this book by writing Discovery House Publishers, P.O. Box 3566, Grand Rapids, MI 49501, U.S.A. For information about other Discovery House books, music, videos, or DVDs, contact us at the same address or call 1-800-653-8333. Find us on the Internet at http://www.dhp.org/ or send e-mail to books@dhp.org.